Winning Low-Limit Hold'em

Lee Jones

W9-AVL-270

ConJelCo titles:

Books

Software

Winning Low-Limit Hold'em

Lee Jones

 ConJelCo
Pittsburgh, Pennsylvania

Winning Low-Limit Hold'em
Copyright © 2000 by Lee Jones

All rights reserved. This book may not be duplicated in any way or stored in an information retrieval system, without the express written consent of the publisher, except in the form of brief excerpts or quotations for the purpose of review. Making copies of this book, or any portion, for any purpose other than your own, is a violation of United States copyright laws.

Publisher's Cataloging-in-Publication Data

Jones, Lee

Winning Low-Limit Hold'em/Lee Jones.
iv, 200 p. : ill. ; 22 cm.
ISBN 1-886070-15-6
I. Title.
Library of Congress Catalog Card Number: 00-108737

Second Edition

9

Cover design by Cheri Soriano and Lisa Lane

The "Bee" Ace of Spades is a registered trademark ® of the United States Playing Card Corporation and is used with their kind permission.

ConJelCo LLC
1460 Bennington Ave.
Pittsburgh, PA 15217-1139
[412] 621-6040
http://www.conjelco.com

Contents

Foreword

T o the list of the writers of great poker manuals — Sklansky and Malmuth, Brunson and Caro — we must now add the name of Lee Jones... For those on the nursery slopes of Hold'em, anxious to get it right before ascending to loftier levels — or those who've had their bankrolls burned at higher altitudes, and can swallow their pride long enough to start the long climb again   Lee has compiled the soundest advice I've ever read. I only hope I can summon the self-discipline to follow it myself. Play Lee Jones's user-friendly system, and you'll soon find yourself earning respect at any table in any card-room in the poker world.

And a whole bunch of bucks better off.

Anthony Holden — author of *Big Deal*
London, England
August 29, 1994

Foreword to the Second Edition

I'm delighted to be asked to write a foreword to the second edition of *Winning Low-Limit Hold'em*. Lee's book has changed the landscape of lower limit hold'em games over the past six years. If you don't know what's in this text, you're playing at a serious disadvantage to those who do. You have to pay for your poker lessons one way or another; *Winning Low-Limit Hold'em* is by far the cheaper tuition plan. Now, let's play hold'em.

Linda Johnson — former Publisher of Card Player
Las Vegas, NV
September, 2000

Who Should Read This Book?

How often have you bought a book only to discover that it wasn't what you were after? Before you spend your money on this book, you should know if it's right for you. So,

Read this book if:

- You have played some poker, but have never played hold'em and you'd like to give it a try. Maybe it just showed up in your Thursday night home game. Maybe you just moved into a town where they have public cardrooms. Maybe you're getting ready for a trip to Las Vegas and want to spend some time playing poker. If you read this book through once, you'll be able to sit down and hold your own in just about any low-limit hold'em game.

- You've been playing hold'em for a month, or a year, or ten years, and you just can't beat it. You see the chips flying around the table, and once in a while you have to borrow a laundry bag to carry your winnings out, but sometimes you have to borrow the laundry bag to cover the upper half of your body. This book will help you find the problems in your game and correct them.

- You're holding your own in low-limit hold'em games. Occasionally, players will get up and leave when they see you sit down. Nevertheless, you think that you might be missing an extra bet or two every session. This book may give you some ideas on how to find that extra bet.

Don't read this book if:

- You've never played poker. If that's the case, then we strongly urge you to buy *Fundamentals of Poker* by Mason Malmuth and Lynne Loomis or *Poker for Dummies* by Richard Harroch and Lou Krieger. Read and start playing. Then come back here and start reading.

- You're routinely crushing the competition in a $30-$60 hold'em game in southern California. You don't need this book. However, we suggest that you frequently review *Hold'em Poker for Advanced Players* by David Sklansky and Mason Malmuth.

We hope you'll find this book worth reading.

♠ ♥ ♦ ♣

Introduction:
Why a Book on Low-Limit Hold'em?

It's not like the world is clamoring for yet another hold'em
book. Furthermore, in our opinion, Sklansky and Malmuth
have written the definitive text on how to play medium-limit
hold'em.

*However, $3-$6 hold'em is probably the single most common
card game in U.S. public cardrooms.* If you have never played
poker in a casino or public cardroom and decide to give it a try,
there's a very good chance you'll find yourself in a $3-$6 Texas
Hold'em game. Also, the low-limit game and its players have a
very different nature from that described in existing literature. In
some parts of the country, they have a special name for this
game: "No Fold'em Hold'em."

What's the difference between low- and high-limit hold'em?

The concepts that you must understand to win at low-limit
hold'em are the same as those for any hold'em game (or any
poker game for that matter). However, many of the strategies
and ideas presented in other texts are not applicable to low-limit
games. This is not because those strategies are wrong, but because they are aimed at higher limit games and tougher opponents.

Why should the correct strategy for a low-limit game be different from a higher limit contest? After all, a $30-$60 game is just
a $3-$6 game played with $10 chips. However, *in general*, the
players in a $30-$60 game are stronger than those in a $3-$6
game. They know more about the game, odds, different plays,
etc. Furthermore, the higher limit players are generally tighter.
Many fewer people will pay to see the flop in a $30-$60 than will
in a $3-$6. Therefore, there are some important strategic differences between the two games.

Perhaps the biggest difference between low and high-limit games can be summed up in a single word: mistakes. In a high-limit game, *most* players will be more experienced. They will make very few fundamental mistakes, and to beat them you will have to make the most of every small edge you get. On the other hand, in low-limit games, your opponents will generally make *many* fundamental mistakes. They will call when they should fold, check when they should bet, etc. Therefore, you don't need to capitalize on small mistakes. You can wait until you have a big advantage (either you have a very strong hand or your opponent has made a serious mistake) and then take maximum advantage of it. For that reason, your "variance" — the up and down swings in your bankroll — may be less than that of an expert player who plays in a tougher game.

I should note that since publishing the first edition of this book, I have seen many of the "low-limit" game conditions we describe in games as large as $15-$30 and $30-$60. Particularly in the California poker communities, many of the amateur players are quite well-off, and some are very wealthy. Just as a rich businessman might choose to play blackjack for $100 per hand with no concept of basic strategy, some well-to-do amateur poker players play $20-$40 hold'em even though they know very little about the game. Of course, in the $20-$40 game, there will probably be a few players who are very good, but remember: you don't have a take a test to play higher limit games.

What will you learn from reading this book?

This book will teach you how to play correctly in those "No Fold'em" games. It will teach you which hands you can play, and which hands you can raise. Perhaps most importantly, it will teach you when to *fold*. We'll cover various skills that you need to beat the low-limit hold'em game. In some places, we'll go a little deeper into the theory — *why* you're making a certain play rather than just *what* to do. You'll later learn that all of this knowledge makes an excellent foundation for moving into bigger and tougher games.

If you read and study this book carefully and then apply what you learn at the tables, you will be able to beat just about any low-limit hold'em game.

What is your goal?

This book will teach you to be a solid low-limit hold'em player. Like the best poker authors before us, we emphasize tight but aggressive play; this means you won't play many hands. You may find *watching* a lot of hands, as opposed to *playing* a lot of hands, boring. If your goal at the poker table is to have fun, do a lot of *gambling*, and catch an occasional miracle card, then you should not follow our recommendations. There is not a thing wrong with this approach to poker; however, you will not be a consistent winner. If that doesn't bother you, and you can afford the cost of your entertainment, we hope you enjoy yourself. On the other hand, if you get your satisfaction from winning the most money in your poker game, then you're on the right track by reading this book.

Note also that your opponents at the table will have different reasons for being at the table as well. Understanding *their* reasons for playing is a powerful tool to help you beat them.

What games does this book cover?

This book covers hold'em games from $1-$2 (becoming increasingly rare) up to $5-$10 or $6-$12. At the $10-$20 level and above, you will need some new skills, and you will see many more solid players than in the lower limits. The example game in this text is a $3-$6 structured limit game (described in detail in "Hold'em Fundamentals" beginning on page 12). Spread limit games are discussed beginning on page 148.

How this book is organized

The text is divided into three major sections. The first section is an overview of the mechanics of hold'em and the types of games you will encounter. The second section is the real meat of the book, describing how to play before the flop, on the flop, and after the flop. Finally, the third section covers miscellaneous topics, including a bibliography of our favorite poker books and a glossary.

We encourage you to read the book from cover to cover at least once, and then to review it (particularly the second section) regularly. You will find that the first few times you play hold'em, most of the advice in the book will flee the moment you sit down at the poker table. And conversely, the first couple of times you read the book, little of it will make sense. But as you go back and forth between the book and the table, each will become more understandable.

Vocabulary

Poker, like most pursuits, has its own vocabulary. We make an effort to introduce terms to you before using them, but if you come across something you don't understand, look it up in the glossary at the back of the book (page 176).

One final caveat

Playing poker *well*, like playing the cello, hitting a good forehand, or writing a clear paragraph, demands study and practice. If these could be done by following a simple formula, many people would do them. However, if you spoke to Yo-Yo Ma, Martina Navratilova, and George Will, they would tell you that they practiced incessantly to master their craft. You might be surprised to learn that the best poker players have probably "practiced" more hours than any of the distinguished people mentioned above.

We have literally worn the bindings off our best poker books reading and rereading them. We have also invested thousands of hours in playing poker. We hope you will do the same on your journey toward poker excellence.

Acknowledgments

While only my name appears as the author, this book could not have been written without the assistance and ideas of Roy Hashimoto. Among other things, he was the first person I've heard formalize the concepts of "implicit collusion" and the "dominated hand" — both incredibly powerful ideas in low-limit poker games. I believe that Roy has extraordinary insight into poker theory; despite pleading from both myself and the publisher, he chose not to have his name appear as a co-author of this book. My frequent use of the editorial "we" is intended to convey Roy's participation in this project.

My experience with low-limit hold'em has been largely gathered at San Francisco Bay area cardrooms, and I am indebted to all the players there, good and bad, who make around-the-clock poker a reality in my town. I also note with delight that as of January 1st, 1998, cardroom poker in California became non-smoking, and we could return to the tables without risking our lungs.

I also need to thank my friends (met and not yet met) on Usenet's rec.gambling (now rec.gambling.poker) and Martin Veneroso's ba-poker list on the Internet for excellent conversations about poker theory and practice. The same holds true for my valued poker buddies at various home games in which I participate.

Chuck Weinstock of ConJelCo unhesitatingly said "Yes" when I suggested a book, even though I'd never before written one — I am grateful for that vote of confidence. I also need to thank all the folks at *Card Player* magazine for their support, assistance, and friendship. Of course, when you mention *Card Player*, you have to mention Linda Johnson in the same breath. Linda has done extraordinary work to promote poker and bring it (sometimes kicking and screaming) into the 21st century[1]. I'm proud to call her a friend. I also avoid any poker table at which she's sitting, except to say "Hi."

Ken Butler, Michael Maurer, and Jay "Sippy" Sipelstein spent many hours reviewing the original manuscript. Their efforts dra-

---

[1]Just as we were preparing to go to press, Linda announced her retirement from *Card Player*.

matically improved its quality. Sandra Bond's copy editing cleaned up a lot of awkward prose.

I have benefitted immeasurably from the great poker writers — you can, too. Read Brunson, Caro, Ciaffone, Krieger, Malmuth, Sklansky, and Zee (see page 173 for a complete list of valuable references). Then reread them.

My first poker lessons (as well as those in craps, roulette, and blackjack) came from my father, who, to the best of my knowledge, has never played any of those games for money. He believed them to be a good way to teach me about numbers, counting, and percentages. My mother, perhaps to counteract this education, gave me an object lesson in gambling while on a camping trip when I was five. Standing in a Nevada laundromat, she showed me a nickel (which I knew to be exchangeable for a candy bar) and dropped it into a slot machine, explaining that I would get no value for the nickel. Of course, the slot machine spewed forth a couple of dollars' worth of nickels. To both of them, I am grateful for gambling lessons, and much more that I can never repay.

Finally, and most importantly, I come to my extraordinary family: Lisa, David, and John Haupert. Lisa and I were married three years ago, and she brought to the marriage David (now 17) and John (now 13). The amount of time it took me to get around to the second edition is simply an indication of how much fun I've been having with them.

Disclaimer

I strongly believe that the information in this book is correct. However, neither I nor any other poker writer can guarantee results at the tables. You, your opponents, and your cards are responsible for that.

LHJ
San Jose, CA — July, 2000

Introduction to the Second Edition

I was wrong. There — I said it. Yes, there were some things in the first edition of this book that needed to be changed. After all, it has been almost six years since the first edition was published. If you study and participate in some activity for that long and don't learn a new thing or two... indeed, if you don't change your mind about some things you thought you knew, then you're not really paying attention, eh?

That said, I believe that the first edition of this book provided a solid foundation for new hold'em players. I have been extremely gratified by the response that the poker community has given to "WLLH"; I can't count the number of letters and emails that I have received from readers telling me how much they learned from the book. If you were one of those correspondents, or anybody who read and enjoyed the book, I thank you. If you were one of the people who pointed out mistakes and told me ways I could make the book better, I thank you even more. With the exception of the gentleman who told me that I needed to cover video poker, I trust that all of you will see your suggestions in print here.

Those of you who read the first edition will notice that the jackpot chapter is gone. I decided I had nothing useful to say about jackpots, and rather than spend a chapter saying that, I'd just say it here and be done with it.

♠   ♥   ◆   ♣

Conventions Used in this Book

Throughout this book, we use the following notation to describe various hold'em hands — both general classes and specific:

Rank   The rank of a card is represented as a single number or upper case letter: A, 2, 3, 4, 5, 6, 7, 8, 9, T, J, Q, K.

Suit   The suits are represented with their symbols: ♣, ◆, ♥, ♠

Starting Cards Two card hold'em starting hands are shown as two character pairs. Since the specific suit doesn't matter, we show whether the two cards are suited or not with a lower case 's' or 'o' ("offsuit"). For example, "T8o" is ten-eight offsuit; "J9s" is jack-nine of the same suit. A card whose rank is unimportant is shown as an 'X'. For instance, AXs is an ace and any other card of the same suit.

Specific Hands Specific hands where suit is important are shown as hyphen-separated pairs. For example, "K♠-9◆" is the king of spades and nine of diamonds; "T♥-T♣" is the ten of hearts and the ten of clubs.

Ranges   Sometimes we will specify a range of hands that you can play before the flop. For instance, we might use the range "KJs-T8s" when talking about hands with a single gap between the rank of the cards. This example would refer to the hands KJs, QTs, J9s, and T8s.

Section I

Hold'em: The Game

Hold'em Fundamentals

Hold'em (or more properly, "Texas Hold'em") is a deceptively simple poker game because only two of the cards you play are exclusively yours. The rest are shared with the other players.

Play of the hand

Each player is dealt two cards face down. These two cards are the only ones that are exclusively his.[1] There is a round of betting. Then the dealer burns a card (discards it face down onto the table) and deals three cards face up in the center of the table. These three cards are called the "flop" — they are community cards that are shared by all players. There is a second round of betting. The dealer burns another card and turns a fourth community card face up. This card is called the "turn." There is a third round of betting. The dealer then burns another card and deals the fifth and final community card face up. This card is called the "river." There is a fourth and final round of betting.

If more than one player is left in the hand after the final round of betting, there is a showdown. Each player makes the best five card poker hand he can using his two hidden cards and the five "board" cards (the flop plus the turn and river). He may use two, one, or zero of his hidden cards to make his hand. If he uses neither of his two cards, he chooses to "play the board," and the best he can do is tie all other remaining players.

Betting formats

There are two common betting formats in limit hold'em:

"Structured" games have a fixed amount that a player may bet or raise on each betting round. Typically, this is the same amount on the first two betting rounds, and then twice that amount on the

---

[1]Throughout this book, we use male pronouns and possessives. This is not an attempt to slight female dealers, players, or readers. The material in this text is difficult enough without confusing the sentence structure.

last two rounds. For instance, a $3-$6 game would have $3 bets and raises before and after the flop, then $6 bets and raises after the turn and river cards. We use this $3-$6 game as an example throughout the book.

"Spread-limit" games permit a player to bet any amount within a certain range on each betting round. For instance, a common spread-limit format is $2-$6, wherein a player may bet or raise as little as $2 or as much as $6 on each betting round. However, a raise must be at least as large as any previous bet or raise in that round. Therefore, if somebody bets $5, any subsequent raise on that betting round must be at least $5. Another common spread-limit format increases the range on later betting rounds. For instance, a $4-$4-$8-$8 game has bets and raises between $1 and $4 on the first two rounds. On the last two betting rounds, players may bet or raise anything from $1 to $8.

Public cardrooms and casinos

In public cardrooms and casinos, hold'em is played with 9 to 11 players. A house dealer sits in the center of one side of a long table. His job is to deal the cards, determine the winner(s) of the hand, collect the house rake or time charge, and run the game. He is *not* a player in the game.

A "dealer button" is placed in front of one player. It is a white acrylic disk labeled "DEALER." The person with the button is the nominal dealer. The cards are dealt starting one to his left, and he acts last on all betting rounds except the first. This player is often referred to as "the button."

Hold'em games rarely have an ante paid by each player. Nevertheless, in any poker game there must be some seed money in the pot. Therefore, the first player to the left of the button puts in a forced bet called a "blind." More specifically, his blind is called the "small blind" and is a fraction of a full bet (typically $1 or $2 in a $3-$6 game). The player to *his* left puts in another forced bet called the "big blind" — a full $3 bet in our example. Spread-limit games often have just a single blind, one position to the left of the button.

Because the first two players have already acted (by putting in blind bets), the player one to the left of the big blind is the first with any choices on the pre-flop betting round. He may fold, call the $3 bet, or raise the bet $3 (now forcing other players to call $6 if they wish to continue). Each player in turn has this choice with one exception: there is a maximum of three or four raises per betting round.[2] Thus, after the maximum number of raises, a player may only call or fold.

The blind bets put in by the first two players are "live blinds." When the action gets back around to them, they have the same choices as the other players except they already have a full or partial bet in the pot. For instance, when the betting gets to the little blind, if there has been no raise and he has posted a $1 blind, he needs to add only $2 to complete his bet. However, he may fold, or raise by putting in $5. The big blind already has a full bet in the pot, and if there has been no raise, he can call without putting more money in, or raise the bet $3 to a total of $6.

On each round of betting after the flop, the player to the left of the button acts first and may either check (choose not to bet) or bet. In the $3-$6 game, he is restricted to betting $3. In a spread-limit game, he may bet any amount in the valid range. The betting round proceeds from there.

When the fourth round of betting is completed (after the river card), the dealer determines the winner of the pot and pushes him the chips. If two or more players have equivalent hands (suits do not matter), the dealer splits the chips equally among them. Then he moves the button one position clockwise, shuffles the deck, and deals the next hand.

---

[2]There is often an exception to the raise limit rule: if only two players are in the pot, they may raise each other until one of them is out of chips.

Time collection and rake

The cardroom has to make money somehow; the two common ways are taking "time" payments and "raking" the pot.

If the house takes "time" payments, it either collects a fixed amount (generally $5-6) from each player every half hour, or requires the player on the button to put up a fixed amount ($3 is common). Either way, the money is removed from the table and dropped down a collection slot by the dealer.

In cardrooms where the pot is raked, the dealer removes a specified amount of money from each pot. A common rake in low-limit games is 10% of the pot, with a maximum of $3 or $4.

Reading the Board

A s a hold'em player, you must be able to read the community cards (the "board") and recognize how your hand compares with other possible hands, in particular, the *best* possible hand (known as the "nuts"). For example, if the board is

the nuts is an ace-high spade flush. If you have A♠-7♠ in your hand, you know that you have the best possible hand and will win the pot. Now the only interesting question is how to get lots of your opponents' money *into* the pot. If you have Q♠-T♠, you have the second best possible hand. Your hand is still very good, but anybody with the A♠ and another spade beats you.

If the board has a pair on it, then a full house or four-of-a-kind ("quads") is possible. For a board of

the absolute nuts is four kings. However, if you have K9 in your hand, the worst that you can do is to split the pot with one other player who has exactly the same hand. You've eliminated the possibility of four kings because you have one, and your kings full of nines is the biggest full house possible.

You need to study many hold'em boards until you can spot the nuts (and the next couple of best hands) almost immediately.

♠ ♥ ♦ ♣

Odds, Pot Odds, and Implied Odds

To play poker well, you must understand the terms *odds*, *pot odds*, and *implied odds*. Let's be sure that you grasp each term thoroughly before we go on.

Probability and odds

"Probability" is the likelihood of an event happening. It is a number between zero and one, and is often expressed as a percentage. For instance, a .70 probability of rain today is the same as a 70% chance of rain.

"Odds" are another way of expressing probability and are more applicable to games of chance such as poker. Odds are shown as a pair of numbers separated by a colon; the pair represents a ratio between the probability of an event happening and its not happening. Being somewhat whimsical, we could say (from our example above) that rain is a 7:3 "favorite" today. That is, the odds of rain are 7:3 in its favor; for every seven times it rains on a day like today, there will be three dry days. The opposite of favorite is "underdog" (or "dog" for short). If you say, "That team is a 5:2 underdog," you mean that for every two times they win in this situation, they will lose five.

What do odds mean to betting? Let's consider the weather forecast above. You and a friend decide to bet on whether it will rain. Given that you know rain is a 7:3 favorite, what is a "fair" bet? If you choose to bet on rain, and your friend bets on no rain, you should put up $7 for each $3 he wagers. Over 10 days, it will probably rain seven times. You will collect $3 from your friend on each rainy day for a total of $21. On the remaining three days, it will not rain. Your friend will collect $7 from you on each dry day for a total of $21. Thus, on any given day, one of you will pay the other, but in the *long run*, you will both expect to break even. Now, suppose you can find somebody willing to put up $4 for each $7 you bet, but you know that rain is indeed a 7:3 favorite. You still lose $21 on the three dry days, but you collect $4

17

each of the seven rainy days for a total of $28. In 10 average days, you make a $7 profit! This book will teach you to find and exploit opportunities where you have a similar edge over your opponents.

Let's look at a hold'em example. Suppose you have flopped a heart flush draw. That is, you have two hearts in your hand, and two more come on the flop. What are the odds of making your flush on the next card (the turn)? There are a total of 13 hearts in the deck; you have seen four of them, leaving nine more. You have seen a total of five cards (your two plus three in the flop). That leaves 47 unseen cards, of which nine are the hearts you want to see. There are 38 cards that do not make your flush and nine that do; the odds are 38:9 "against." You are a 38:9 (slightly worse than 4:1) underdog to make your flush on the turn.

Pot odds

Pot odds are the odds being offered to you by the pot compared to the amount of money you must invest in it. For instance, suppose after the river card is turned up, there is $30 in the pot. Your opponent bets $6. The pot now has $36 in it, and you have to call $6 to see his hand. You are getting *pot odds* of 6:1. You will also hear the expression "the pot is *laying* you 6:1." Now your choice is (relatively) easy: if you are no worse than a 6:1 underdog to win the pot, you call the $6; otherwise you fold.

Pot odds also apply to draws. Suppose you have a draw that is a 3:1 underdog to be made. For you to call a bet, there should be at least three times as much money in the pot as the amount you must call. Of course, that includes any bets that precede your call. For instance, if the pot contains $15 and your opponent bets $6, the pot now contains $21 and is laying you 3.5:1. Since you are only a 3:1 underdog, you can call.

Implied odds

Going a step beyond pot odds are *implied odds*. More accurately, they might be called implied pot odds. When you compute pot odds, you can only consider the money that's already in the pot.

The concept of implied odds lets you ask the question, "If I make the hand I'm drawing to, how much more money will I win than what's already in the pot?"

For example, suppose you have a flush draw with one card left to come. You know you are about a 4:1 underdog to make your flush. There is $16 in the pot, and your opponent bets $6. The pot (now $22) is laying you about 3.7:1, but you're a 4:1 dog to make your flush. According to strict pot odds, you can't call. However, suppose you're "sure" that your opponent will call a $6 bet on the river if you make your flush. Now you can act as if the pot contains $28 (what it currently contains plus the $6 more you will win if you make your flush). You can make the $6 call with your flush draw.

Of course, when considering pot odds or implied odds for a draw, you must be "sure" that you will win the pot if you make your draw. If you're not sure, then the pot must lay you a higher price to make your draw correct. Also, when considering implied odds, you must be just as sure that your opponent will call your bet after you have made your hand.

Your money, the pot's money

Poker players often get confused about to whom money belongs. They say, "I have a lot of money in the pot." This is a fallacious concept. Once the money is in the pot, you should no longer care whether it came from your stack or those of your opponents. The only interesting question is whether the pot is laying you the correct price for a draw or whatever.

Don't worry about how much money you have contributed to a pot during a hand when deciding if a call is correct. The pot odds (or implied odds) will answer that question and are unaffected by your past contributions to the pot.

Some odds you should know

You are a 220:1 dog to be dealt a pair of aces (or any other specific pair). You are a 16:1 dog to be dealt a pocket pair.

You are a 3.3:1 dog to be dealt two suited cards.

You are a 7.5:1 underdog to flop trips if you hold a pocket pair.

If you have an ace and a king in your hand, you are a 2.1:1 underdog to flop at least one ace or king.

If you have a pair of pocket kings, it's about 4:1 in your favor against a single ace showing on the flop without a king.

If you have two suited cards, you are a 7.5:1 dog to get at least two more of your suit on the flop.

If you flop a flush draw (four to a flush), you are a 4.2:1 dog to make your flush on the turn. You're a 4.1:1 dog to make it on the river if you don't make it on the turn (you've seen one more card that's not your suit). Once you've flopped four to a flush, you're a 1.9:1 dog to make it by the river.

If you flop an open end straight flush draw (e.g., you have T♠-9♠ and the flop comes 8♠-7♠-2♣), you are a 1.2:1 *favorite* to make a straight or better by the river.

An open end straight draw is about a 4.9:1 dog on *either* the turn or the river. If you flop an open end straight draw, you are a 2.2:1 underdog to make it by the river. With a gutshot (inside) straight draw, you are an 11:1 dog to make your straight on the next card.

Computing odds

Computing your odds of making a draw on the next card is fairly straightforward. You simply compare the number of cards that don't make your draw to the number that do. Those are your odds. For instance, suppose you have J♥-9♥ and the flop comes T♦-5♠-Q♣. Any eight or king will give you a straight[1]; you have eight outs[2]. What are the odds of making your straight on the next card? Of 47 unseen cards, eight make your straight, 39

---

[1]It's worth noting that the straight you make with the king is not the nuts. Be sure you know what *is* the nuts.

[2]An "out" is a card that will make your hand, and presumably win the pot for you. This term, and many others, are defined in the glossary.

do not. Thus you are a 39:8 (almost 5:1) underdog to make the straight on the turn.

♠　　　　♥　　　　♦　　　　♣

The Typical Low-limit Hold'em Game

When you sit down in a low-limit hold'em game, you are likely to find a broad range of poker experience and knowledge. Some players will be retirees who use the game as their social club and book fifty hours or more there each week. Others will have a discreet crib sheet in front of them showing the ranking of poker hands. Most of your opponents will lie somewhere in between — they'll be working folks who come down to the club for relaxation and a good poker game.

Low-limit games are often only half-jokingly called "no fold'em hold'em." You will often see seven or eight people at a nine-person table call to see the flop. Furthermore, many players will stay around after the flop with very weak or almost hopeless draws. In some cases, they *know* that they're taking the worst of the odds, but they get a special charge from catching those miracle cards and beating very strong hands.

Unlike in higher limit games, you are not likely to encounter any professional players in your low-limit hold'em game; your opponents will be playing for entertainment. The most obvious result of this is that people want to play more hands.

The two most common kinds of games are "loose-passive" and "loose-aggressive."[1] In the former, many players pay to see the flop, but there is not much raising. In the latter scenario, there are many players for each flop, but many pots have three or four bets put in before the flop — everybody is "gambling." Note that the common thread between these two types of low-limit games is many players in each pot; this is unusual in higher limit games.

Sometimes the nature of the game will change, and it will get much tighter. When somebody raises before the flop, he may win the pot right there. A significant percentage of hands do not

---

[1]See the chapter "Player Stereotypes" beginning on page 140 for more information about these terms.

go past the flop. This is most common in short-handed games (ones with fewer than the regular number of players).

Quiz on Preliminary Chapters

Congratulations! You've made it through the first section. To help cement the important points in your mind, please take this quiz, and *write down the answers*. Then check your answers against the answers on page 26. If you get any answers wrong, go back and re-read the text until you understand the answer to each question.

1. Should you read this book if you've never played poker?

2. What level of games do we define as "low-limit"?

3. How many cards in a hold'em hand are uniquely yours?

4. How many betting rounds are there in a hold'em hand, and when do they take place?

5. How many cards does the "flop" contain?

6. How many cards do you use from your unique cards to make your best five card poker hand?

7. Under the conventions of this book, what hold'em hands do the following represent?
   a) 88
   b) QJo
   c) T9s
   d) AXo
   e) J♠-T♣
   f) K♦-4♦
   g) AQs-J9s

8. What is the best possible hand (the "nuts") given these boards? What is the second best possible hand?
   a) A♦-K♥-6♠-4♠-T♣
   b) 7♥-4♠-3♦-9♥-J♠
   c) A♣-5♠-T♥-2♣-9♠

d)   3♣-J♣-Q♥-6♣-3♦

e)   6♦-9♦-9♥-K♠-5♦

f)   T♣-5♥-J♦-Q♠-K♣

g)   J♠-2♣-Q♦-4♥-7♣

h)   4♥-6♠-8♥-J♦-9♥

9.   Suppose you have the hand 8♥-8♦. On the turn, the board is 6♣-8♠-7♦-9♥. What are your odds of making a full house or better on the river?

10. From the previous question, suppose just you and a single opponent are left in the pot on the turn. He bets $6, and you are persuaded that he has a straight. Of course, if you make a full house (or better), you will win the pot. How much money has to be in the pot after he bets for your call to be correct?

11. Suppose you believe that your opponent will check and call your $6 bet if you *do* make a full house. Then how much money should be in the pot for you to call, trying to make a full house or quads?

♠   ♥   ♦   ♣
_____

Answers to Quiz on Preliminary Chapters

1. No, you should read *Fundamentals of Poker* by Malmuth and Loomis, or *Poker for Dummies* by Harroch and Krieger first.

2. $1-$2 up through $5-$10 or $6-$12. Spread-limit games from $1-$3 up to $2-$10.

3. Two.

4. Four. Pre-flop, after the flop, after the turn, after the river.

5. Three.

6. Two, one, or zero. If you use zero, the best you can do is split the pot with all players remaining in the hand.

7. a) A pair of 8's.

   b) A queen and a jack of different suits (offsuit).

   c) A ten and a nine of the same suit (suited).

   d) An ace and any other card of a different suit.

   e) The jack of spades and the ten of clubs.

   f) The king of diamonds and the four of diamonds.

   g) The range of suited one-gap hands including ace-queen suited, king-jack suited, queen-ten suited, and jack-nine suited.

8. a) QJ for the ace high straight; next best is three aces.

   b) T8 for the jack high straight; next best is 56 for the seven high straight.

   c) 34 for the five high straight; next best is three aces.

   d) Four threes; next best is queens full of threes.

   e) 8♦-7♦ for the nine high straight-flush; next best is four nines.

   f) Any ace for the ace high straight; next best is any nine for the king high straight.

g) Three queens; next best is three jacks. Note: three queens is the lowest possible hand that can be the nuts when all five board cards are dealt.

h) A♥ and any other heart for the ace high heart flush; next best is K♥ and another heart for the king high flush.

9.   To improve to a full house or better, you need the board to pair. There are three each of sixes, sevens, and nines, plus the last eight in the deck. That makes a total of ten "outs" that give you a full house or better. Since you've seen six cards (two in your hand, four on the board), there are 46 unseen cards, ten of them good for you. Thus your odds of improving (making a full house or quads) on the river are 36:10 (3.6:1) against.

10.   You are about a 3.6:1 underdog when your opponent bets $6. Thus for you to call the $6 bet, the pot must contain 3.6 x $6 (about $22) when you call. If the pot (including his last bet) is at least $22, you can call, hoping to improve on the river. If you want to squeak out the last statistical detail, note that for your opponent to have a straight, he must have either a five or a ten. Because that five or ten must be in your opponent's hand, you can remove it from your theoretical deck of remaining cards. Now you can say that you have 10 outs from 45 (instead of 46) unseen cards, making you a 3.5:1 underdog. The pot must contain $21 for you to call.[1]

11.   If you are persuaded your opponent will call your $6 bet on the river, that is an extra $6 you plan to win should you improve. You are still a 3.5:1 dog, so you still need $21 total to justify your call. Subtracting the extra $6 you plan to win, the pot only had to contain $15 for you to call on the

---

[1]Believe me, this is right. It's also not at all intuitive, and not the least bit necessary to worry about until you start posting on Internet poker forums.

turn. Note: All these calculations were done assuming you would throw away your trips on the river if you didn't improve. If you were planning to call a bet if you *didn't* make your full house, then you are effectively calling $12 ($6 on the turn and $6 on the river). Now the pot has to be offering you better odds to call on the turn.

Section II

Play of the Hand from Deal to Showdown

Playing Considerations Before the Flop

This chapter is not going to be easy.

There, you're warned. This is the first chapter in which we actually talk about *how* to play low-limit hold'em. You will have to read, study, and re-read this chapter and many others in the book to get full value from them. It will be difficult, but it will be rewarding.

Your decision to call, raise, or fold before the flop must be based on several factors. Among the most important are:

- Your cards
- Your position
- Your relative position
- How much money you must invest initially
- The number of players in the hand.
- How your opponents play

If you ignore *any* of these factors when making your first playing decision, you are not likely to be a winning hold'em player.

Your cards

Starting hands (the two cards that are unique to your hand) in hold'em fall into some natural categories. You will learn that hands in different categories do well in different situations, so you need to understand and remember these categories.

Pocket Pairs: two cards that are a pair, for example, "pocket 9's." Since the difference in value between pocket aces and pocket deuces is so huge, we will separate the pocket pairs into three sub-categories: aces down through jacks are "big" pairs, tens through sevens are "medium," and sixes through twos are "little" pocket pairs. These subcategories are, of course, somewhat arbitrary, but this is a reasonable division.

Big Cards: two "big" cards, ace through jack. A♣-Q♦ and K♥-J♦ are examples of *offsuit* big cards. A♥-K♥ and K♠-Q♠ are examples of *suited* big cards.

Connectors: two cards one apart in rank. They have the ability to make straights and, if suited, flushes and straight flushes. Examples are T♦-9♦ and 6♣-5♠. Note that QJs has the distinction of being both "Big Cards" and a "Suited Connector." We sometimes include in this group the lesser quality hands with gaps between the ranks. For instance, 9♠-7♠ is a suited "one-gap." T♣-7♣ is a suited "two-gap."

Suited Aces and Kings: fairly self-explanatory. Examples are A♠-8♠, K♥-9♥. Of course, a suited ace is much stronger than a suited king because if you make a flush with it, you have the nut flush, whereas the king high flush can be beaten by the ace high flush. Having an ace high flush is *much* better than having a king high flush. Having a king high flush is only a *little* better than having a queen high flush.

Believe it or not, even if you chose to play only hands that are in these categories, you would be playing too many hands. Some of them are not strong enough to play in certain positions and some of them (32s comes to mind) are generally not strong enough to play *anywhere*. However, many of your opponents will play every hand that fits into the above categories, and a lot more as well.

Your position

Your position is simply where you are in relation to the button. Being on the button is the best position because you will act last in all but the first betting round. Being one to the left of the button is then the worst position.

Position is perhaps the most undervalued[1] component of good hold'em play. It's easy to see that bigger cards are better, suited is better than non-suited, and if there is raising going on, you need a stronger hand to play. However, many (if not most) low-limit hold'em players make their playing decisions without considering their position. *If you play without careful attention to your position, your bankroll will suffer.*

By acting after other players, you know what they will do (check, bet, etc.) before they know what you will do on a given betting round; this gives you an advantage. For instance, suppose you have a very strong hand. If your opponent acts before you and bets, then you raise. If he checks, you bet. Regardless of his action, you get the maximum amount of money in the pot. On the other hand, if you're first to act, then you must decide between betting immediately, hoping he will call, or trying to check-raise. If you check with the intent of raising and he checks too, you have lost the bet you would have made had you bet and he called.

Here's another example of the importance of position. Suppose you have 55 as your starting hand. If you are the first to act before the flop, you normally shouldn't call. We will cover this in detail shortly, but you need a lot of opponents to play small pairs. Suppose you call with your 55 in early position. If the next player to your left raises and scares out the other players, you now wish you hadn't called the original bet. However, suppose you are on the button. If somebody raises early and limits the pot to two players, you fold, knowing you're doing the right thing. But if six players call in front of you and there's no raise, you can call with your fives. Simply being closer to the button means you have more information about how many opponents you will have and how much you'll have to invest, enabling you to play this hand.

---

[1]That is, position is very undervalued by the average recreational player. Strong hold'em players base their game heavily on position, almost as much as on the cards they play.

There is one aspect of position that is perhaps not as important in low-limit hold'em as it is in the higher limits. In tough hold'em games, when the flop doesn't hit[2] anybody, the player last to act can often bet and win the pot immediately. Because of the number of "calling stations" that are often in a lower limit game, it's unlikely you'll be able to do that. However, good position is still vitally important, and you must consider it at all times.

For the purposes of this text, we will consider a nine-player table. We'll declare the first four positions to the left of the button "early position," the next three "middle position," and the last two (including the button) "late position." Of course, you'll need to adjust this for the exact number of players at your table. When doing so, tend to err on the side of caution; if you can't decide if it's early or middle position, call it "early."

Your relative position

There is another aspect of position to consider — let's call it "relative position." It is where you sit in relation to specific other players at the table. Obviously, your position with respect to the button will change as it moves around the table. Your relative position to another player will be less volatile. For instance, if you sit immediately on a player's left, then you'll act after him on every hand with the exception of ones on which he has the button. If you sit directly opposite him at the table, you will act before and after him equally often.

If there is a player who is very aggressive and raises a lot, you'd generally like to be to his left. That way, you'll see those raises coming before you act and can drop your marginal hands. If you sit to his right, too often you call one bet only to have him raise behind you and now you wish you'd saved the first bet.

---

[2]The flop is said to "hit" you if it contains cards you can use. If you have A♠-K♠ and the flop comes A♦-7♣-4♥, it has hit you. If it comes Q♠-J♠-10♦, it has clobbered you over the head. If it comes 8♥-7♥-6♥, it has missed you completely.

If, however, that player bets and raises almost always (let's say 90-95% of the time), then you want to have him on *your* left. Because he'll be initiating action so frequently by betting or raising, you'll effectively act last after he has started the action. For instance, this gives you the opportunity to check-raise the entire table when you make a strong hand. Remember, for this to be correct, that particular opponent must be almost guaranteed to bet or raise when given the chance. Otherwise, keep him to your right.

In general, you'd like to have loose passive players to your left. They behave predictably so you're more willing to have them act after you. You will have an easier time predicting what they'll do, and will make the right play more often.

You may even want to move into an empty seat that gives you better position with respect to certain players.[3]

Note: positional concepts are not easy but they are important. After you've read the entire book, come back and read this section again — it will probably make more sense.

How much money you must invest initially

The obvious reason a player raises is that he has a strong hand. If you are playing in a pot that has been raised one or more times, there is a much better chance that you are up against strong hands, and are more likely to make a second best hand. You need a stronger hand to play in a raised pot.

Also, lots of raising before the flop reduces your implied odds. As we discussed before, that's money not currently in the pot that you plan to win if you make your desired hand. As an example, consider playing a small pair before the flop. You call with the pair, hoping to flop a set.[4] If you don't flop a set, you will fold. You would like to pay one bet rather than four to see the

---

[3]Mason Malmuth's book *Gambling Theory and Other Topics* contains an excellent discussion of where you want to sit in relation to various kinds of players.

flop with this hand. The amount of money you'll win after the flop (assuming you make your set) will be about the same regardless of the amount you invested pre-flop. Thus, if you must call lots of raises pre-flop, you are paying a higher percentage of your anticipated earnings before you've made your hand.

You must consider the possibility of a raise *behind* you when deciding what to play. This is one of the reasons that position is so vitally important. When you decide to play a hand before the flop, you *know* only what has happened in front of you. You have to suspect/guess what is going to happen behind you and play accordingly. Obviously, if you have reason to believe that there will be one or more raises behind you, you need a stronger hand to play.

The number of players in the hand

Again, this is a widely ignored factor, which you are *not* going to ignore.

Certain kinds of hands do well against a small number of opponents. These are hands that can win a pot with little or no help from the board — big pocket pairs and big cards. With a pair of pocket kings, you can often win a pot, betting all the way, without improving that pair. However, as the number of players in the hand goes up, you run a much larger chance of having a little two pair or freak straight beat you. The same holds true for AK, but you probably need to get an ace or king on the flop.

Conversely, some hands are "drawing" hands and need significant help from the board. However, if that help comes, they can turn into very big hands that you are happy to play against a lot of players. For instance, A♦-7♦ is not a very good hand on its own. Even if an ace flops, you could be in big trouble because of your low kicker. However, if you make a diamond flush, it's the nuts if there isn't a pair on the board,[5] and you're delighted to

---

[4]A "set" is a pair in your hand and a third card of that rank on the board. It is still three of a kind, but this is more desirable than three of a kind where two of your rank are on the board.

have lots of company in the hand with you. Since these drawing hands need help that comes somewhat rarely (for instance, with a suited ace you will only flop two more of your suit about 11% of the time), you need lots of players in the hand to provide the pot odds to call.

Thus, in general you'd like to play your big cards and high pairs against a small number of players and your smaller pairs and suited cards against many opponents.

How your opponents play

You have to know something about how your opponents play to play your cards optimally. For instance, suppose there is a player on your immediate right, and he hasn't played a hand in 20 minutes. He's currently under the gun (first to act before the flop) and he raises. You have KQo — what do you do? You fold. Suppose, however, that the player on your right has raised the last eight straight hands. He raises for the ninth straight time (again, under the gun) and you have the same KQo. What do you do? You might well re-raise here. Concepts such as this are crucial if you want to succeed at poker.

Playing behind a raiser

You'll see that I recommend playing very tightly behind a raiser, even one who raises too much. Many players who would be winning players are losers because they call too many raises cold. So, the mantra for what to do when it's raised in front of you: "I'm looking for a reason to get out of this hand."

Last action

This is another crucially important concept, not only pre-flop, but on every betting round. If your calling a bet will end the betting round, you can play much more liberally than you can oth-

---

[5]For the nit-picking reader, it is true that the ace high flush can be beaten on an unpaired board if somebody makes a straight flush. One takes one's chances.

erwise. This is simply because you don't have to fear raises behind you. For instance, you have 7♣–5♣ on the big blind. The first person in raises, and gets three callers. It's fine for you to call there because you "close the betting."[6] But if the action went call, call, raise, call, and now it's your turn, you should usually fold. The first two callers will *almost* always just call the second bet, but when one of them decides to re-raise, you're paying too much for your hand pre-flop. And if the original raiser makes it four bets, you have a miserable situation.

When you're thinking about calling (on *any* betting round) with a marginal hand, be much more willing to do so if you have last action.

Summary

We've discussed the important factors you must consider when you decide whether to get involved in a pot. In the next four chapters, we'll cover what you can play pre-flop and how to play it. As you read those chapters, refer back to this one to see how the decisions are based on the above considerations.

Changes in the second edition

I've made some pretty substantial changes in the starting hand requirements for the second edition. These reflect my playing experience over the past six years, and, perhaps more important-ly, input from some extremely good hold'em players[7]. In partic-ular, I've learned a lot about starting hand requirements from Abdul Jalib[8], who has done excellent simulations with Bob Wil-son's Turbo Texas Hold'em software.

---

[6]To the best of my knowledge, Mike Caro publicly coined this term.

[7]I won't name them all here. They know who they are and don't need the pub-licity.

[8]At this writing (summer of 2000), Abdul's musings on poker can be found at www.posev.com. Not everybody agrees with this "simple desert nomad," but I find the rationale and logic of many of his arguments compelling.

But it's important to understand that this set of starting hand requirements is just a beginning. Honestly, I don't believe it matters much whether you follow this set of starting hands, Sklansky and Malmuth, Krieger, or any other intelligent poker writer. The areas in which the various writers disagree probably account for a tiny fraction of your results, either way. For instance, I don't think it will affect your long-term results a great deal if you do or don't play QTs for a single bet in moderately early position. Of course, in the short term, you might flop a costly second-best hand with it, or turn a monster-crushing straight flush, but over the course of your poker career, I doubt you'd be able to tell financially whether you played it three from the big blind or not. On the other hand, if you choose to play J6o there, or don't routinely get a lot of money in the pot with KK in that position, your results will suffer dramatically.

Also, game conditions can dramatically affect what you should play where. If a good hold'em player is asked, "Can you play AJo in early position?" the answer will be, "It depends." On how well his opponents play, how tight they are, what the current texture of the game is, his table image, and so on.

So, treat all of starting hand information as guidelines and not gospel. If in doubt, fold — another hand will be along shortly, and you may well be avoiding an expensive mistake.

Be extra conservative if you're a novice

When you're new to any sport or activity, you start out slowly and become more adventurous as you gain experience and knowledge. Hold'em is no different. When you're first learning the game, avoid the lower end of any of the hand rankings. For instance, you'll see that I say you can play 64s and 53s in late position if enough players are in. If you're new at this, don't bother. You can make plenty of money *not* playing them, and they may cost you money when you're still in the beginning stages of your hold'em career.

Playing Pre-Flop in Early Position

*You must play very tightly before the flop
in early position.*

If there is no raise in front of you

You can play any of the big or medium pocket pairs in early position. With AA-JJ (and occasionally TT), raise — you have a very big hand. However, against eight random hands, your pocket aces will end up the best hand only about 35% of the time. Don't feel bad about that; if you got pocket aces on every hand (and your opponents forgot this after every hand), you would make a ton of money.

With TT-77, usually just *call*. The traditional reason for raising with these pairs is to reduce the number of opponents, particularly those holding a single ace or king. If raising is effective at thinning the field in your game, by all means do so. However, in low-limit games, you probably won't have much success getting singleton aces and kings to fold for a raise. Therefore, it makes more sense to see the flop cheaply.

In early position, you want unpaired cards to be huge. Raise with AKs-KQs, AQs, AJs, AKo, and AQo.

In the previous edition, I was hesitant recommending a raise with AK (suited or not). That was a mistake. You should raise with AK simply because it figures to be the best hand out (against anything but AA and KK, you're no worse than even money). However, as you'll see in the chapter on playing the flop, you will normally need to improve your AK to win the pot.

There aren't many non-pairs that you should call with in early position. You can call with KJs, QJs, and as your position improves, JTs and KQo. You can also call with ATs and A9s.

A word about AJo: when you're new to the game, I encourage you to fold AJo in early position. Interestingly, raising AJo in early position is generally a bad idea. You might make hands worse than yours (e.g. AT, A9) fold, but you'll never make hands better than yours (AK, AQ) fold. So you're limiting the opposition to those hands better than yours. Conversely, if your raise doesn't cause people to fold (because they're loose players), then you're playing an unsuited two-gap hand against a large field, out of position. Another bad situation. So you can't raise with it, and calling with a marginal hand (which AJo is) in early position is not how you win money. Until you have the experience to know when you can sneak in with AJo, dump it. Note the significant difference between this hand and AJs or AQo.

If the game is loose and passive, you can shade these requirements down a little with your pairs and suited hands. For instance, it would probably be okay to call with 66-55.

If there is a raise in front of you

The key idea here: "Look for a reason to fold." Even if the raiser is a hyper-aggressive lunatic, (1) hyper-aggressive lunatics get dealt KK on occasion, and (2) if somebody is holding KK behind you, you're going to be facing a third bet. So, play *very* tightly behind an early position raiser. Reraise with AA-JJ, AKs, AKo. Maybe AQs and AQo. Call with TT and AJs.

Again, remember that you won't have to wait long for the next hand. And while you're waiting for that next hand, ponder this sobering thought: it's almost *always* a mistake to call an early position raise with KQo.

Be patient

Following these guidelines, you will play only about 1 in 12 hands you get in early position. If the game is loose-passive, then you will play about one in seven hands. Be patient and wait for the best cards; your early position handicap demands that you do so.

Summary — early position

Raise: AA-JJ (sometimes TT). AKs-KQs, AQs, AJs, AKo, and AQo. Always re-raise with AA-JJ.

Re-raise with the others in this group if it will tend to limit the number of players in the pot.

Call: TT-77, KJs, QJs-JTs, ATs, A9s, KQo.

Fold: Everything else.

Remember: You must play *very* tightly before the flop in early position.

Playing Pre-Flop in Middle Position

As your position improves, you can start to play a few more hands, but you still have to be conservative in what you play.

Of course, you can play anything that was playable from early position.

If there is no raise in front of you

Pocket pairs: You can play them down to 6's or 5's. If the game is loose-passive, you can play any pair. Raise down to 99 or 88 and call with the rest.

Big cards: You can raise with the same hands you would have raised in early position, plus a few others — KJs, QJs, ATs, KQo, AJo, ATo. You can call with KJo and QJo-JTo.

Suited connectors: You'd like to play those against a large number of opponents since you probably need to make a straight or a flush to win. If there are three or four players in the pot before it gets to you, you can call with suited connectors down to 98s. The more callers, the lower you can go. You can also play the suited one-gaps QTs and J9s. Again, if there are just one or two players in the pot, you need to tighten up, playing only those suited connectors that have big card value too.

If you're in a loose-passive game, you can call with any suited connector down to 76s and suited one-gaps to T8s.

Unsuited connectors: I am now persuaded by Abdul Jalib's simulations and my own experience that unsuited connectors are not as valuable as some people feel[1]. Therefore, don't get involved with unsuited connectors unless they have big card value too.

That said, I want to make special mention of JT. Either suited or unsuited, it has some unique properties: it makes the most possi-

---

[1]To quote Abdul, "A hold'em player cannot live by straight draws alone."

ble straights, all the straights it makes are the nuts, and when you make a straight with it you often get lots of action. That's because it makes straights with high cards, and beats big pairs, two pairs, and even sets. Don't call raises cold with it, but with a couple of people in, it's a good hand to play for one bet. Note: T9o is *much* weaker than JTo.

Suited aces and kings: If you have a few callers in front of you, you can call with AXs. Your suited ace will flop a flush draw (or flush) almost exactly as often as your pocket pair will turn into trips on the flop. You need plenty of people in the pot to make this call correct. You can play suited kings down to about K9s or K8s. When playing these hands, remember that if the flop comes ace-high or king-high you have top pair, but might also have kicker problems — be careful.

If there is a raise in front of you

Just as in early position, you need to tighten up considerably. Not only do you have to put in two bets, you must also consider the possibility of a re-raise behind you. You can generally just go back to early position rules for hands that you can call. However, you can play pairs and big suited connectors if it's clear that enough players (4-5) will be in the pot to justify it.

Reraise with the same hands that we suggested re-raising with in early position. These are very big hands that justify putting more money in the pot on pure expected value.

If the pot has been raised twice or more before it gets to you, there are a couple of things to consider. First, there's a good chance that the betting will be capped. Second, you're up against at least one, if not two, big hands. Go back to those early position premium hands and rely on them. For example, you can quickly throw away pocket 10's unless there are already five or six players in.

Once again, if there's a raise in front of you, look for a reason to fold.

If you're the first one in

While this is relatively rare in most low-limit games, it's worth mentioning. If you're the first one in, particularly if you're just two off the button, you have some chance of winning the pot before the flop with a raise — "stealing the blinds." Many players will defend their blinds with any two cards, and if that's true, then you shouldn't raise any more than usual. But if the players in the blinds will sometimes fold to a raise, and you're the first one in, then raise any hand you were going to play anyway. Don't play more hands than you would have otherwise, but if you have a chance to steal the blinds, don't call — raise.

Summary — middle position

<u>Three or fewer callers in front</u>

Raise:	AA-88, AKs-QJs, AQs-KJs, AJs, ATs, AKo-KQo, AQo, AJo, ATo.
Call:	77-55, JTs-98s, QTs-J9s, AXs, KXs (to K8s), KJo, QJo-JTo.

<u>Four or more callers in front</u>

Raise:	Same as above
Call:	Above plus 44-22, 87s-76s, T8s, K7s.

<u>A raise in front</u>

Raise:	AA-JJ, AKs, AQs, AKo, AQo.
Call:	TT-99, KQs-QJs, KJs, AJs. If a few players are already in, 88-77, ATs.

<u>Chance to steal blinds</u>

Raise:	Any hand you were going to play anyway.
Fold:	Everything else — don't call.

Playing Pre-Flop in Late Position

When you are in the last couple of positions to act, you have an extraordinary advantage.

This is where you can take some liberties with the hands you play. Remember, in a typical low-limit game, by the time the action gets to you a lot of players will already be in the pot. In many games, you'll be the seventh or eighth player to get his money in.

Now you can play more speculative hands. Furthermore, you'll act last (or second to last) in every succeeding betting round. You can take some chances here, because you'll see how the betting is going before you have to act.

If there is no raise in front of you

Pairs: Given that five or six players have called and nobody has raised, play *any* pocket pair. Again, raise with AA-88, otherwise call and look at the flop. If you like the flop (nothing bigger than your pair) or love the flop (you make a set), everybody has to act in front of you, and you'll be holding the big hand. Realize that particularly for hands such as 99 and 88, you may well need to flop a set to win with them. But you're getting the right price and you're punishing players who have limped in with junk.

Big cards: You can play just about any two big cards. However, remember that your unsuited big cards do *not* like lots of opponents. You can call with QJo after a lot of people are in the pot, but you want the flop to hit you pretty hard. Even if you flop top pair with that hand, you run the risk of an overcard falling later, and you may already be up against two pair. However, your position gives you license to play some borderline hands. Call and see how you like the flop.

Suited connectors: These are the kind of hands you like to play in late position. You can play suited connectors right down to 54s. Even the one-gaps down to about 75s and two-gaps down to about 96s are ok. Of course, you need plenty of people in the pot with you, but that will usually be the case. Again, stay away from unsuited connectors that don't have high card value, or JTo, as I discussed previously.

The thing to remember is that you're going to need real help on the flop with these hands, and it's not going to come very often. Most of the time you play these hands, you'll be throwing them away on thc flop. However, once in a while you will flop a big hand or draw with them.

Suited aces and kings: You can play any suited ace or king in the last two positions if you have a few callers in front and no raises. However, you must treat them like the suited connectors — if you're holding A7s, and flop just an ace, you will have to play it very delicately. What you're really hoping for on the flop is a big flush draw (or pat flush). On the button, you can even play suited queens if there are a bunch of loose callers in front of you.

If there is a raise in front of you

Playing from last position, you'll have a pretty good idea of the effect of the raise. If the raise happened in early position but a bunch of people have called it already, you know that the pot will lay you proper odds for your drawing hands. If the raise happens in late position after a lot of calls, you're probably still okay since very few players will call one bet and then throw their cards away for a single raise.[1]

You're going to get tired of hearing me say this, but I'll say it again: if there's a raise in front of you, look for an excuse to get rid of your cards. If you wouldn't call a raise cold with it in middle position, don't call a raise cold with it in late position. However, you'll get to play a few more hands because you'll have a better idea of how many opponents you'll have.

---

[1]This intuitive behavior — to call a single raise after you've already committed one bet — is generally correct. At that point, the pot is laying you a very high price for a single bet (assuming you don't fear a re-raise).

Stealing the blinds

As you reach the last position before the button and the button itself, if you're the first person in, and you're going to play, raise. This may win the blinds for you; it may get you the button. At the very least, it will put your opponents on the defensive, and that's always desirable.

Again, do not take this as liberty to open-raise with anything on the button. Throw away J6o without a second thought unless the blinds don't defend enough, in which case you should open-raise with any two cards. But that's usually not the case in low limit games. Normally, they'll defend too much, so you should throw away your weaker hands and punish their looseness by raising with your better ones.

Also note: a hand in which a late position player open-raises and just the big blind defends is a very different beast from a typical multi-way pot. Any pair or draw is a pretty good hand, and top pair is a monster. This sort of hand-to-hand combat is not for most poker novices. It's more art than science, and until you're ready to learn that aspect of the game you might be better off folding all but your very big hands if you're the first person in on the button.

Summary — late position

<u>Four or fewer callers in front</u>

Raise:	AA-88, AKs-QJs, AQs-KJs, AJs, ATs, A9s, A8s, AKo-KQo, AQo, AJo, ATo, A9o.
Call:	77-55, JTs-54s, QTs-75s, AXs, KXs, QJo-JTo, KJo-QTo, KTo.

<u>Five or more callers in front</u>

Raise:	Same as above
Call:	As above, plus 44-22, 64s-53s, QXs.

<u>A raise in front</u>

Raise:	AA-JJ, AKs, AQs, AKo, AQo

Call: TT-99, KQs-QJs, KJs, AJs. If a few players
                       are already in, 88-77, ATs, A9s.

Chance to steal blinds

Raise: The higher range of anything you were going
                       to play anyway.

Fold: Everything else — don't call.

Note: I've made every attempt to make the starting hand tables
consistent. However, if you find an inconsistency, here's the rule:
if you can play it in early position, then you can play it in middle
or late position. If you can play it in middle position, then you
can play it in late position.

Playing Pre-Flop in the Blind Positions

Being in the blind positions puts you in an awkward situation. You already have all or part of a bet in the pot, so you must pay less to enter the pot and you are being offered better pot odds to participate. However, you are in the worst position for the rest of the hand.

Big blind

This one is somewhat easier to consider because you already have a full bet in the pot. If there is no raise, you can see the flop for "free." Thus the important questions are when to call a raise and when to raise.

You will see many players "protect" their big blinds irrationally — don't be guilty of this. Don't call with Q7 or 84 or other such trash hands. Your blind money is already in the pot — don't vainly chase after it with money you're not *required* to put in. On the other hand, be aware of those players at your table who *will* protect their blinds to extremes. Don't try to steal blinds from those players with a late position raise, but do punish their need to protect hands that should be thrown away.

Raising from the big blind

In the first edition, I encouraged you not to raise much in the blinds. I now believe it's correct to raise simply because you probably have the best hand, and this punishes people who limped in with trash. However, many times after the flop, you have to abandon the hand you raised with simply because it didn't get enough of the flop and it's obvious that somebody else did. Raise with AA-88, AKs-QJs, AQs-KJs, AKo-KQo, AQo.

Defending the big blind against a raise

Quite often you are getting truly huge pot odds — 10:1 or better — when you're in the big blind and there's a single raise. That means that you can play a lot of hands as long as you have cards that can flop a big hand. Any pair, any suited ace, king, or queen, any suited connector or suited one-gap. Avoid unsuited cards unless they're big. Your real danger of defending with something like A7o is that you're up against a better ace, and flopping an ace is only going to cost you money.

If it's two bets cold to you, forget all the above — look for a reason to fold.

Little blind

Depending on how much of a bet the little blind is, you can be fairly liberal in what you play. For instance, in $2-$4 games, the little blind is typically $1 — half a bet. You can call with any reasonable hand: any two suited cards, any connectors down to about 54o, any ace, any king. Still, throw away the trash such as J2 and T4.

If your little blind is only a third of a bet (which is often the case in $3-$6 and $6-$12 games), you need to be tighter. Furthermore, don't forget that you have to act first for the rest of the hand. In rare cases the little blind is two-thirds of a bet.[1] In that case, play just about any two cards (assuming there's no raise, of course).

If there's a raise in front of you, you can largely discount your current investment in the pot. Play it as if you were in middle position and had a raise in front. If your hand could play there, go ahead and call.

Guidelines for raising in the little blind are about the same as in the big blind. The big difference is that you may want to raise or re-raise to knock the big blind out and isolate yourself against one or two players whom you think you're ahead of (or can outplay after the flop).

---

[1]This is actually quite common as you get into higher limit games ($15-$30 and above). In those games, the little blind is almost always 1/2 or 2/3 of a bet.

Chopping the blinds

Sometimes two players sitting next to each other will agree to "chop" the blinds. That is, if everybody folds in front of them, each will simply take his blind money back and they won't play out the hand.

In general, I recommend against doing this. If you're a better player than your opponents, then you have the edge and should take advantage of it. Also, it gives you practice in the crucially important skill of playing heads-up.

There are, however, two exceptions to that. First, some clubs have a "no flop, no drop" policy in which they don't remove any money from the pot if there's no flop. Many players agree to chop the blinds if such a policy is in effect, and it might be best to go along with it. Second, if you will seriously offend your opponents by refusing to chop, you might want to do it just for your table image. However, most players don't get upset about a player who refuses to chop as long as he's consistent one way or the other.

Free play on the button

In some clubs, the time payment is taken on the button but acts as a blind bet. In those circumstances, you're almost *forced* to play. You have the best position and part or all of a bet in. For instance, suppose the time payment of $2 is taken on the button, but acts as a blind bet in your $3-$6 game. In that case you should call with any two cards. You can call a raise with any hand that would have called a single bet for full price. Since your pot odds are essentially doubled (everybody else is putting in two bets while you're putting in 1.3 bets), you can call a single raise very liberally.

Trash Hands and How to Avoid Them

Texas Hold'em took California by storm in 1987. One of the reasons for its great popularity:

Any two cards can win.

Why, if you had 72, the flop could come all deuces![1]

While many players have learned that playing hands like 72 is a quick way to get rid of your poker bankroll, many have not, or have not learned the lesson very well. Perhaps the most important lesson we can teach you in this book is how to recognize trash hands and get rid of them.

The "dominated" hand

We define a "dominated" hand as one that will virtually *always* lose to another better hand. Even if that better hand does not win, the dominated hand will consistently come in behind.

For instance, consider

If you flop a king with it, you have top pair. However, if you have more than one or two opponents in the pot with you, you run a good chance of being out-kicked (somebody has a king with a better kicker). The only real hope for your hand is a miracle flop like 3-3-x or K-3-x. If the flop comes K-K-x, you probably have the best hand, but nobody is going to call you on that flop unless they can beat you. Time after time you'll get shown KT, KQ, etc.

---

[1] And it does — about once every 19,600 flops.

Furthermore, if even you *do* have the best hand, you can't win much money with it. Suppose you have K3 and flop top pair (i.e., the flop comes king high). If you bet and are called, you dare not bet again, because the caller probably has you beaten. If the caller doesn't have you beaten, he probably won't call again. Thus, the best you can do with a dominated hand is win a tiny pot.

Note: in some circumstances we suggest that you can call before the flop with any suited ace, and in some cases, any suited king. However, you're really looking to flop your flush draw (or maybe two pair). If you flop just the ace or king, you have a problem.

Other weak hands

Generally, two-gap and three-gap hands just aren't worth the trouble. Three-gaps are especially bad. For instance, with

you can only make one straight (5-6-7-8-9), and it's not the nuts. If the flop comes nine high, you've got no kicker, and you're vulnerable to overcards.

Small pairs played in the wrong circumstances are bad as well. For instance, with a pair of 4's, you're a tiny statistical favorite over AKs, but where are you going with it? Unless you flop trips, you don't know which card beats you. Your opponent could have AK, AQ, KJ, etc. He could have a small (but larger than your) pocket pair, in which case you're a huge underdog.

Plain trash

There are some hands that you will see played routinely in your low-limit game. You will also occasionally see those hands drag big pots: Hands like 83s, T4o, J6o, 52s, etc. *If you play hands like this regularly, you will lose all your money.* It is that simple.

If you want to play hold'em for entertainment only, and you consider your losses the cost of your entertainment, then go ahead and play trash hands. Otherwise, you must throw them away.

Summary — Trash

Suited faces: QXs, JXs, etc., except where they are specifically mentioned

Two and three gaps: Q9, Q8, J8, J7, etc., except in very special cases (mentioned elsewhere)

Pseudo-high cards: KX, QX, JX, TX

Random suited cards: 94s, T3s, etc.

Random cards: T2o, 84o, etc.

Deception in Pre-Flop Play

D eception is a fundamental part of poker. You want your opponents to think you're weak when you're strong, and you want them to think you have the nuts when you have nothing. Unfortunately, this goes against what you'd like to do in general: bet and raise with good hands, and minimize your investment in the pot with bad ones.

Deception has varying degrees of importance depending on the poker game you're in. If you're in a big money no-limit hold'em game, deception may play an enormous role. However, in a low-limit hold'em game,

You will usually have to show your opponents the best hand to win the pot.

The two main reasons for this are:

1.   In low-limit games, with many players contesting each pot, it's difficult to represent a big hand that you don't have. Either some other player is already looking at that hand, or somebody will call you, almost out of curiosity.

2.   Deceiving your opponent requires that your opponent be giving some thought to what you have. Often, your opponent is simply playing *his* cards and hasn't really thought about what *you* have.

For instance, in higher limit games, you can often raise with

before the flop against just one or two players. Then if the flop misses everybody, your bet will probably win the pot immediately, even against somebody that has flopped bottom pair.

However, in a low-limit game, you probably have at least four or five opponents. The probability that the flop missed *everybody* is much lower. Furthermore, the fellow who made bottom pair may decide to call you all the way to the river.

Therefore, deception does not play the role in low-limit hold'em that it does in other games.

Places that deception is useful

Now that we've said all that, we'll discuss where a little deception *is* worthwhile. Just remember that a large percentage of the time you should do the obvious thing.

One deceptive strategy is the "limp-reraise," which is akin to the check-raise after the flop. Since you can't check before the flop, you simply call with a powerful hand and then re-raise when there's a raise behind you. This can be a very powerful play if there's a lot of pre-flop raising going on and you're almost sure that there will be a raise behind you. If you're going to limp-reraise, do it with your biggest hands — huge pairs, AKs, AQs. But you have to do it when you have an almost iron clad guarantee that somebody behind you will raise, allowing you to re-raise. If you're at all unsure, do the raising yourself, and then put in a fourth bet if it's re-raised behind you.

With hands that do better against a lot of opponents (medium pairs, connectors), you can occasionally raise when you know that you have the number of opponents you need. For instance, you can raise with

on the button after a lot of people have called. This mixes up the normal raising that you do with your big pairs and connectors.

Don't waste your big hands

There are two basic versions of deception — playing big hands slowly, and playing small hands fast. Don't waste your big hands by playing them slowly. They are infrequent enough as it is, so when you get one, look for a way to put lots of money in the pot. If you feel the need to be deceptive once in a while, play a small hand (one that can flop big) fast.

The Pre-flop Raising War

Sometimes an entire table will seem to go on tilt. Pot after pot is capped before the flop. The presence of a couple of maniacs or a player on tilt can be the catalyst for this event.

When this happens, many of the players are doing their gambling before the flop. They'll happily put in four bets with

and hope the flop comes 7-7-5 or 3-4-6 or whatever.

In these circumstances, you must hunker down and play very tightly. Throw away hands such as ATo and QJo. You want to play big pocket pairs and big suited connectors — starting hands that can turn into monsters with the right flop. The probability of just top pair getting out of such a hand alive is painfully low — everybody is going to stick around to catch that second pair or inside straight. That said, realize that top pair with a big kicker is how you make your money in hold'em, and this is no exception. Take your chances and take your lumps, but when you have AKs and flop K-7-2, that's *your* flop - play it accordingly.

Understand that raising wars can make your bankroll go through wild swings. You end up paying four or five bets before the flop, and then if the flop hits you the least little bit, you're stuck in there because the pot is so huge.[1] However, winning just one or two of those pots can make you a big winner for the night (or the week).

---

[1]With all the pre-flop bets in the pot, you are getting correct pot odds to stay for some pretty wild draws such as backdoor flushes and inside straights. This further increases your investment in a long-shot pot.

Remember, when the table gets on tilt, play only your strongest quality hands, and be prepared to go through some rough sailing with them.

And that's all

In the first edition, I referenced Roy Hashimoto's suggestion that you could also profit simply by playing a little tighter than wild and crazy opponents. That may be true, but I haven't seen evidence of it. Furthermore, it seems that most low limit opponents will let you play only premium cards, and yet still give you action when you show up in a hand.

Therefore, I am removing the equivocal language from this chapter. When the table gets crazy, play only your best cards; you'll get the money in the long run.

Quiz on Pre-Flop Play

1. What are the four most important factors to consider when deciding how to play your starting two cards?

2. Define the following terms:
    a) pocket pair
    b) big cards
    c) connectors
    d) one-gap
    e) suited ace

3. Would you prefer to play AKo against two players or seven players?

4. Would you prefer to play 77 against three players or seven players?

5. Define early, middle, and late position.

6. Which pocket pairs can you play in early position, regardless of game conditions? Which pairs can you play if you're in a loose-passive game?

7. Can you play KTo in early position?

8. You are in early position and find yourself holding 98s. Under what circumstances can you play this hand?

9. Under what circumstances can you play a suited ace in middle position?

10. You have 76s in middle position. There is one caller in front of you. The player to your left has raised the last three pots pre-flop. What should you do?

11. You have 54s in middle position. There has been very little raising in your game, and an average of six or seven players taking the flop. Three players call in front of you. What should you do?

12. You are on the button with T8s. Three players call. What do you do? Now consider the same question if the third player raises instead of calls.

13. Suppose you are one in front of the button. Four players have called in front of you. Would you prefer to have KJo or JTs?

14. You have 33 on the big blind. Three players call, and the button raises. What should you do?

15. You have AK on the big blind. Five players call, and nobody raises. What should you do?

16. You have 74s on the button. In this game, the button pays a time charge equal to the big blind, and the time charge plays for you as a bet. There is a raise and two cold calls in front of you. What should you do?

17. You have KK in early position. What percentage of the time best describes how often you would raise (rather than call) with this hand: 90%, 50%, or 10%?

18. You have JTs in middle position. What percentage of the time best describes how often you would raise (rather than call) with this hand: 90%, 50%, or 10%?

19. You are in late position with AJo. The last five pots have had the pre-flop betting capped. It's been raised twice before it gets to you. What should you do? Suppose you had AJs instead of AJo. What should you do?

20. Define a *dominated* hand and give an example.

21. Under what circumstances would you play Q3o or T5s?

Answers to Quiz on Pre-flop Play

1. Your cards, your position, the number of players in the pot, and the number of bets required to see the flop.

2. a) pocket pair — two starting cards of the same rank. Examples: QQ, 77.

    b) big cards — two starting cards ten or greater. Examples: AJs, KQo.

    c) connectors — two cards one apart in rank. Examples: T9s, 76.

    d) one-gap — two cards with a single gap in their ranks. Examples: J9s, 86.

    e) suited ace — ace and another card of the same suit. Example: A8s.

3. You would prefer to play AKo against two players. Big cards that are trying to hit top pair with big kicker or two pair do better against fewer players. You may even win the pot with the "nut no-pair."

4. You would prefer to play 77 against seven players. With only three opponents, you are not getting sufficient pot odds to hit a set, and it's difficult to tell if your unimproved pair is best. However, with seven opponents you are getting the right odds (including implied odds) to flop a set.

5. In a nine-person game, early position is the first four positions to the left of the button. Middle position is the next three positions. Late position is the last two positions, including the button.

6. You can always play AA-77. If the game is loose-passive, you can probably play 66 and 55.

7. Don't play KTo in early position.

8. If you are in a loose-passive game (many callers, little raising), you can play 98s in early position. If there is a lot of

raising going on, even with a lot of players, you should not be playing 98s that early.

9.   If you have two or three callers (but no raise) in front of you, and you have little reason to suspect a raise behind you.

10.   You have to fold 76s here. There is too good a chance that the person to your left will raise again, and limit the field. You want a lot of players in the pot if you're going to play small suited connectors. Also, you'd rather not pay two bets to see the flop with this hand.

11.   In this situation, you can call with 54s. Unlike the situation in the previous question, you are likely to have enough opponents to make your call correct, and you anticipate seeing the flop for only one bet.

12.   If there are three callers and no raise in front of you, T8s is an easy call on the button. If the third player raises instead of calling, you should fold T8s.

13.   If there are four callers in front, you would rather have JTs, which is a drawing hand and plays better against a large number of opponents. If there were only one caller, you'd much rather have KJo.

14.   Assuming the other players call, you will be getting 9:1 to call here. You are only about an 8:1 underdog to flop your set — you can call without hesitation.

15.   Raise. This is a different answer from the first edition, but you almost definitely have the best hand, and your raise pounds on players who limped in with bad hands. Realize that the flop may change everything, but you've put more money in the pot with the best hand, and that's the way to win at poker.

16.   This is probably worth a call. You have perfect position, and what looks like a ragged flop could hit you very hard.

17.   Raise with the kings at least 90% of the time. An alternative way to vary your play is to pick one specific combination (such as "the red kings") and smooth call with those. That would have you raising with them 83% of the time. If there's a raise behind you, re-raise *every* time.

18.   With this drawing hand you don't want to chase players out. Don't raise with this hand more than about 10% of the time.

19.   Fold AJo here without a second thought. If you had AJs, the call would be much less questionable. However, you're probably going to have to make a flush or two pair to win the pot.

20.   A dominated hand is one that is often beaten by better cards, even when it appears to hit the flop. That is, the "good" hand you most frequently make with it often runs into a better hand. Examples: K3 (if you flop top pair you have no kicker), and A6 (same problem).

21.   When you can see the flop for free (you're in the big blind or have posted) or almost free (e.g. a little blind that's most of a bet).

Introduction to Play on the Flop

The flop is the most crucial juncture of the hand.

B efore the flop, you will be playing high quality hands. Your opponents, however, will often be playing all kinds of hands: good, mediocre, and bad. Unfortunately, the value of hands can change dramatically on the flop. Suppose you have

and your opponent has

Let's look at the various odds:

Before the flop: You are a 2:1 favorite

Flop is Q♦-9♥-2♣:   You are a 3:1 favorite

Flop is Q♦-8♥-2♣:   He is a 3.2:1 favorite

Flop is Q♦-8♠-2♣:   He is a 2.5:1 favorite[1]

Flop is Q♠-8♠-2♣:   You are even money (1:1)

Flop is A♦-6♥-2♥:   You are a 15:1 favorite

Flop is A♦-8♥-2♣:   You are a 4:1 favorite

Flop is Q♦-8♥-7♣:   He is a 19:1 favorite

Flop is A♦-K♣-2♥:   You are a 164:1 favorite

---

[1]Note how much your chances improve just by getting one card toward your flush.

Note two important points here. First, even though AKs is a much better hand than 87, if the 87 gets help on the flop and the AKs doesn't, the previously weaker hand is now a substantial favorite. The second point is that in all other scenarios, you are a big (or almost unbeatable) favorite. Thus we see that the flop creates a sharp distinction between the favorite and the underdog.

As we discussed in previous chapters, many players will stay after the flop, even when they are huge underdogs. For instance, if the flop comes

some of your opponents will call a bet (or even two) with 87, hoping to catch another eight or a seven.

On the other hand, you have to realize that your good hands can suddenly become poor ones on the flop. For instance, suppose you have four opponents and the flop is Q♦-9♥-8♥. Your A♠-K♠, which was probably the best hand before the flop, is now almost worthless and should be abandoned if there's a bet.

You want to recognize *on the flop* whether you are the favorite or the underdog, and play (or fold) accordingly. If you call a bet or raise when you don't have the best hand or a good draw,[2] you are giving away money. Conversely, when you have the best hand, you want to maximize the amount of money that goes into the pot. This causes your opponents to make the biggest possible mistakes when they call your bets and raises. As we said at the

---

[2]By "good" draw, we mean one that is correct given the pot odds (or implied odds). For instance, an inside straight draw to the nuts is a good draw only when the pot is fairly large.

beginning of the book, you make most of your money in low-limit games by capitalizing on your opponents' serious mistakes.

Unfortunately, there is a problem. Because the pots in low-limit games are often huge before the flop, your opponents may be correct in calling bets on the flop because of the enormous pot odds they're getting. In the next chapter, we discuss how to deal with that problem — how to coerce your opponents into making big mistakes.

Using the flop to get information

The flop is also a good time to probe for information. In structured-limit games, bets and raises are cheaper here than they are on the next two rounds. You can often risk a small bet on the flop that will enable you to make the correct decision later in the hand when more money is at stake.

For instance, suppose you have a pair of pocket kings and raise before the flop, limiting the pot to you and two other players. Alas, the flop has an ace in it. In this situation, it's usually best to bet immediately on the flop. If you are called, you at least know that you are probably up against a pair of aces (or better) and can play accordingly. If you check, you show weakness and your opponents will probably bet at you on the turn. This puts you into an unpleasant guessing situation. An assertive bet on the flop might well have prevented the opposing bet on the turn, and told you what you needed to know.

♠   ♥   ♦   ♣

The Importance of the Check-Raise

A check-raise is simply checking and then raising when there is a bet behind you. We cannot overstate its importance in low-limit hold'em games.[1]

Why is it so important?

As we discussed previously, the pot will normally be quite large on the flop because there are many callers pre-flop. Furthermore, these players *want* to call your bets on the flop — they did not come down to the card club to fold! Assuming you have the best hand, you now have two possible scenarios:

1. If you have an *excellent* hand — one that is unlikely to be beaten, regardless of the turn and river cards — you are happy to have all these people calling your bets and raises.

2. If you have a *good* hand — one that is probably best right now, but susceptible to being beaten — you would like to eliminate as many opponents as possible. This, of course, is the much more common scenario.

The combination of a large pot and people's desire to call puts you in a bad situation when you have a good, but beatable, hand. Your opponents' instinct (which is to call a lot) *coincides with correct play.* That is, it may be correct for them to call your bet because the pot is large, but they are calling in part simply because they want to call.

Suppose, however, we make your opponents pay two bets rather than one to continue playing. Now, even with a relatively large pot, they may be making a serious mathematical mistake by calling. As we have said before, this is how you make your money at low-limit hold'em.

---

[1] You will occasionally hear people say that check-raising (also known as "sandbagging") is improper or unethical poker. This is absurd. Without it, the positional advantage in hold'em (and some other games) is overwhelming. Cheating and unethical poker playing are despicable; check-raising is neither.

A classic example

You are on the big blind with

There are three callers, and then a raise in late position. You (correctly) call the raise. Now the flop comes

At this point, you suspect you have the best hand. However, if you bet out immediately, you will be putting the *11th* bet into the pot, making it correct for hands such as 98 and 65 to call. Opponents with those hands might well call anyway, but you want them to make a *mistake* by calling when they're not getting sufficient pot odds. Now suppose you check, and it's checked to the pre-flop raiser. When he bets, you raise; the players in the middle have to call two bets cold. Instead of getting 11:1 pot odds, the player directly behind you is getting only 13:2. If he has 98 or 65, he may decide to fold rather than call two bets. If he chooses to call, *you make money* because the pot odds do not justify his call.

But suppose you check, and the person immediately to your left bets. Now some people call, and then you raise. If the original bettor re-raises, the other players are forced to call two (more) bets cold — another mistake. If the bettor doesn't re-raise, the other players are getting correct odds to call the raise. Nevertheless, the net effect is that you get a lot of money into the pot when you are a big favorite and your opponents have weak draws.

Another advantage — the free card

You will find that your opponents in low-limit hold'em will not be as observant as those in higher limit games. However, most people remember being check-raised. If you use the check-raise often on the flop, some of your opponents will become hesitant to bet into you for fear of being check-raised. This can be a significant advantage for you, as in the following example. You call in middle position with

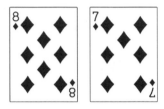

and the flop comes

Everybody, including you, checks to the player on the button. If he bets, you can't call because you didn't get any of the flop. However, he remembers your check-raising him twice during this session, so he checks his A5, and the turn comes

Now you are happy to call a bet on the turn as you have picked up an open-end straight-flush draw! Admittedly, this is an exceptional case (you caught the best card you could have hoped

for), but any time you get a free card with a hand that couldn't call a bet, you have gained a significant advantage. In this case, the specter of your check-raising got you the free card.

The problem with the check-raise

When you decide to check-raise, you must be fairly sure that somebody behind you will bet. If you check with the intent of raising but nobody bets, a terrible thing has happened: you have *given* a free card. This is another reason why you have to watch and study your opponents. In the first example above, you would really like to check-raise. However, if the alternatives are betting out immediately or having it checked around the table, then you should of course bet.

Sometimes the reputation that you get for check raising works to your disadvantage — people are unwilling to bet for fear that you will check-raise! This is good when you have a bad hand with which you'd like to get a free card. It's bad when you have a good hand and want to check-raise. Since you could use a free card more often than you have a check-raising hand, it's OK that your opponents are intimidated. However, if your check-raise is to work, you must be confident that at least one of your opponents is prepared to bet.

Note: in a very small number of public cardrooms and casinos, check-raising is not permitted. It is also prohibited in some home games. If so, your only potent weapon to use up front is gone. You must play *extremely* tightly in front, and bet all your good hands immediately. Hold'em without the check-raise is a crippled game.

Playing When You Flop a Pair

When you flop top pair with a good kicker

This is generally a very good flop for you. Suppose you have raised with

in late position, four other players have called, and there has been no other raise. The flop comes

You probably have the best hand right now. However, there are a lot of things than can go wrong. If the turn card is

you will have to fold if there's any substantial action. Therefore, you want to raise immediately on the flop, and make it expensive for flush draws and overcards to stick around. Even if the board is less threatening (for instance, J♦-6♥-3♣), you still want to raise on the flop. This may get out hands like KQ, which you would like to do. If it's checked to you, bet.

If you're in early position and you get the first flop, you have a problem. You would like to check-raise, but you must be *very* sure that somebody will bet. You definitely don't want to give a free card to somebody with KQ or two hearts. If somebody in late position raised before the flop, he may well bet on the flop, giving you the opportunity to check-raise. If you are the first person to act after the raiser, this would be a perfect time to check-raise, as you have a good chance of making it a heads-up contest.

If you were the preflop raiser, be more inclined to bet (rather than check-raise) on the flop if the flop hits you. Being the preflop raiser, you're almost expected to bet, and this gives you the chance to re-raise if somebody raises behind you.

Note that if you have K♣–J♦ and the flop comes K♦-8♥-3♣, the check-raise is an excellent play because you aren't afraid of an overcard (except an ace) on the turn. If it's checked around, that's unfortunate, but not likely to be catastrophic. It may also confuse your opponents when you bet on the turn. For instance, if the turn is the T♦, somebody with a ten may call you both on the turn and the river, not believing you have the king.

Let's return to the situation where you have A♣-J♣ and the flop is J♦-9♥-2♥. If you raise and are re-raised (or bet and are raised), you must decide how to continue. If you think that raising again will limit the pot to you and the raiser, it may be worth re-raising, even if you suspect he has you beaten right now. By eliminating the other players, you are giving yourself a better shot to win the pot (even though it will cost you an extra bet here). For instance, many players would stay in here with a hand like Q♥-9♦. For one bet, that would not be a terrible play. However, if you re-raise and force that person to call two bets cold, he will probably fold. By knocking him out, you save the pot for yourself if a queen, nine, or two more hearts fall.

If you don't think you can eliminate other players or you are sure that the raiser has a strong hand, you can back off — call the raise and then check and call to the river. It will be difficult to fold in this situation unless the third flush card hits or a king or queen hits. If your opponent continues to bet into you then, you might think about dropping. However, if you call a bet on the turn, you must be absolutely sure of your opponent if you decide to fold on the river. By that time, the pot will be quite large, and you will be making a *catastrophic* mistake if you fold incorrectly. We are not urging you to call *every* bet on the river. Nevertheless, an incorrect fold in this situation can be very expensive, depending on how badly you mis-estimate the odds that you are beaten versus the pot odds.

When you flop top pair with a medium/bad kicker

The most common way this can happen is when you have AXs, hoping to get a flush draw, and just an ace flops. For instance, you have

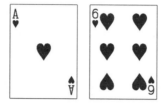

one in front of the button. Five people call in front of you, you call, and then the button calls. Now the flop comes

You have flopped top pair, but you can't like it very much. You have six opponents, and if any of them has an ace, you are probably out-kicked.[1] In a situation like this, if there is much action, you will have to get out. Sometimes when you get out, you will later discover that you had the best hand on the flop, but that will be the exception. If there is a bet and raise in front of you, you

---

[1] Note that if somebody has AT, you're drawing almost dead. That is, since your opponent already has two pair and his lower pair is higher than your kicker, you need two running sixes to win the pot.

should probably drop right there and save yourself further anguish. If there is a bet and a lot of callers, the decision is less clear, but you should probably still fold.

If there is a bet and you are first to act after the bettor (players between you folded or the bettor is on your immediate right), you might want to raise. This is a positional raise designed to get you a free card. On your best days, everybody but the original bettor will fold, and he will check to you on the turn. You then check as well. You hope that he will continue to check on the river, but you should probably call a bet if he bets on the end. If the bettor re-raises on the flop, you can probably drop your hand right then.

Note that we did not recommend *calling* in this situation. This is an excellent example of tight-aggressive play. Either get out, or use your position to get a free card if possible. There is one exception to this. If the bettor is a maniac or a habitual bluffer, you might do well to simply call all the way. If he is bluffing, you will win more money by letting him continue to believe his bluff might work. If he has a better hand, then you lose less by not raising.

If you are in late position and it's checked to you, go ahead and bet, but hope that all your opponents fold. If not, maybe you'll gain a free turn card. If you're called on the flop, prepare to check all the way from there. If you check the turn and somebody bets on the river, you should probably call if the board doesn't look too scary.

If you are in early position with such a hand,[2] you may simply have to check and fold if there is significant action behind you. You have no position to use, and you cannot be the least bit sure you have the best hand. If everybody checks on the flop and the turn is not threatening, go ahead and bet, hoping to win the pot right there. If you are called, check on the river and hope the hand is checked through. However, you probably want to call a

---

[2]We hope you had a free play in the big blind.

bet on the river in this situation. Many of your opponents will automatically bet top pair on the flop and assume you will, too. Since you didn't bet on the flop, they will assume that second pair is good (or may be bluffing completely).

If you are raised on the turn, you can probably fold (note that it will cost you two big bets to get to the showdown now).

This whole discussion points out perfectly our concept of the dominated hand. You will be sorely tempted to call bets (and raises) all the way to the river with your top-pair-no-kicker hand, and yet time after time you will get shown a pair of aces with a better kicker. In the long run, *especially* against many opponents, you will come out ahead by dropping that hand as soon as it misses its flush draw. Note that if you get one of your flush cards on the flop, you are in a different situation. Suppose you have

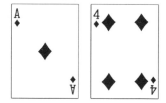

and call on the button after six others have called. If the flop is

you should call a bet on the flop. If the turn is a diamond, you have picked up the nut flush draw, and can easily call a bet.[3] If you do not pick up your flush draw (or otherwise improve) on

---

[3]Sklansky and Malmuth suggest raising on the turn in this situation as a semi-bluff. This is a powerful play in tight games. However, against most players in a low-limit game, this play will be futile as they will almost never fold.

the turn, you are back to the earlier situation and probably have to drop.

An alternative in the above situation is to raise on the flop, and then plan to check the turn. Once you've done that, you will probably need to call a bet on the river, as your check on the turn may well induce somebody to bet.

When you flop second or bottom pair

Normally, it's best to check and fold when you flop second pair. In a low-limit game, this decision is even easier because you are up against many opponents, and at least one of them will have top pair or better.

Let's consider the exceptions. The first requirement is that the pot be large, but in low-limit games that is often true. To continue playing you must also have an overcard kicker (your unpaired card is higher than any card on the board) and/or backdoor draws. For example, suppose you have A♠-T♠, and the flop comes K♥-T♣-4♠. You have second pair, with an overcard kicker, and three to the nut flush. If the pot is big, you can call a bet on the flop, hoping to catch an ace, ten, or spade on the turn.

Note that you should usually *not* call a bet with T♠-9♠ if the flop is K♥-T♣-4♦. Now you have neither an overcard nor a backdoor shot at a flush. If the 4♦ was the 4♠, giving you three to your flush, you are about a 3.4:1 dog to somebody with AK, but some of your outs involve drawing again on the turn. Given that you may make your two pair or flush and still get beaten, you should be getting at least 12:1 odds to call in this situation.

The answer is even more clear cut if you flop only bottom pair. Unless the pot is huge, and you have the secondary outs described above, save your money and fold.

When your pocket pair doesn't improve

If you have a pocket pair that is an overpair on the flop, you have an excellent hand. You can beat top pair with *any* kicker. Treat this as you would top pair on the flop, but you can be even more aggressive. For example, suppose you have Q♥-Q♦ and the flop comes J♣-7♣-2♥. Now if you bet and are raised, you should probably make it three bets. You can beat AJ or KJ (which most people would raise with), and if somebody has a club flush draw, you want to make him pay dearly to stay with it.

You have the same problem deciding whether to bet out or check-raise when you have flopped an overpair. This is not the same as when you have AJ and the flop comes jack high; in that case you are afraid of a king or a queen falling. If you have pocket jacks, and the flop comes nine high, you are afraid of a king, queen, *or* ace. Now you must be that much more sure that somebody will bet if you want to check-raise.

If your pocket pair is *not* the top pair after the flop, you can usually drop it. You are a 23:1 dog to make your set on the turn, so the pot odds (or implied odds) must be that high if you don't have the best hand or other draws. This is not impossible, but it is rare — even in loose low-limit games. Also realize that the betting that made the pot so big may indicate that you're drawing dead. For instance, suppose you have QQ, five players put four bets each into the pot before the flop, and the flop comes ace high. There's a chance somebody has flopped a set of aces, and turning your third queen is only going to cost you a lot of money.

Knowing what card you want

When deciding how to play your top pair (or any hand for that matter), you need to be clear about what you want. For instance, if you have

and the flop comes

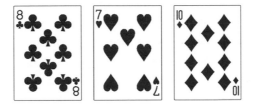

you don't want to make two pair — if a jack falls, any opponent with a nine has a straight. On the other hand, a nine on the turn is probably a very good card for you. So, when figuring which cards improve your hand, only count those that you would truly like to see come up next.

Playing When You Flop Two Pair

Note that initially we are discussing a *split* two pair — when you have two different ranks in your hand, and you flop one of each of them. We will discuss the "pair on the board" situation later in this chapter.

Two pair is a powerful hand that you can play quite strongly. However, it is rarely strong enough to slow play. If you are playing quality hands, your two cards will be close to each other in rank (AXs being the obvious exception). That means that if you flop two pair you have to worry about a straight draw, if not a made straight. Adding the possibility of a flush draw, you have a hand that demands to be played fast; you need to reduce the odds for drawing hands.

When you flop top two pair

Suppose you have

and the flop comes

You can be almost certain that you have the best hand right now.[1] However, you are susceptible to lots of draws. You are essentially even money with somebody who has

Remember also that in low-limit games, the pot has already gotten big. You should do whatever you think will get the most money in the pot on the flop. If you think that a player behind you will raise, bet out immediately and hope you get to re-raise. If you think somebody will bet but not raise, check-raise. Of course, this is a situation where you don't want to give a free card, so if there's any doubt in your mind, bet.

If somebody puts in a third or fourth raise on the flop, you need to consider the possibility that he has a set. Now it might be correct to check and call on the turn and river. If you put in the last raise on the flop, you can bet this hand all the way to the end if the board is not threatening. For instance, suppose the final board is J♣-T♥-5♥-8♦-7♥. You should definitely bet when the 8♦ hits on the turn, but the 7♥ on the river is a terrifying card, as any nine makes a straight, and a flush is possible. You should check, and call if there is no raise. If there's a raise, you'd have to fold here.

Even if the flop is J♣-T♥-7♥ (which makes a straight possible), you should play this hand aggressively. If somebody has a straight, he will probably let you know it quickly (he will be afraid of the flush draw as well). Again, in this situation, you can back off and just call bets. The board will have to become very scary before you should drop this hand.

---

[1]If you don't, there's not much to do. You will lose some money with this hand if it gets beaten, but far more often you're going to win money with it.

When you flop "top and bottom" or bottom two pair

These hands are still strong, but they are vulnerable to the board pairing and draws. Suppose you have

And the flop comes

If another queen hits, you have just about nothing (but can at least fold with a clear conscience). Therefore, it's all the more important that you get your bets in on the flop. Also, don't be so eager to re-raise a second or third time as you would with top two pair. In the situation above, you'd like to believe that nobody was playing Q7o, but in low-limit hold'em, your opponents will routinely show you that (and Q6o, too).

As we discussed before, you should normally be playing cards that are fairly close in rank. Thus, you won't be flopping top and bottom pair too often, with the occasional exception of AXs. When you flop two pair with that hand, play it fast. Many low-limit players will play any hand that contains an ace, and you could quite conceivably be up against the other two aces. If that's the case, you can make a lot of money, and you don't want to give them free cards with which to make a bigger two pair or pair the middle card on the flop. This also insures that you'll be charging the straight and flush draws as much as possible.

Two pair with a pair on the board

This situation is far less desirable than a split two pair. For instance, you have raised with

and the flop comes

Unfortunately, in low-limit games, many players are willing to play almost *any* two cards, so it's hard to figure the probability of somebody having an eight. There is one obvious consideration — the more opponents you have, the more likely it is that one of them has flopped trips. If the entire table takes the flop, and there's lots of action, you must get out. While you may have the best hand, you can't play it with any degree of certainty, and somebody with an eight may just wait and then check-raise you on the river.

In the above situation, it's worthwhile for you to bet on the flop, hoping to win the pot right there. However, if you get called, you have to slow down. You could be up against somebody with a ten, which is fine, but you also may have run into an eight. You should now check on the turn, but be prepared to call a bet on the river. Somebody may represent an eight and you can catch the bluff, but don't give somebody who really *does* have an eight the opportunity to raise you on the expensive bets.[2] Note that betting on the turn and river is a lose-lose situation for you. If you have the best hand, nobody can call you (for fear of the third eight). If you *don't* have the best hand, you'll get called or raised. If you bet the flop, and check the turn, you should be prepared to call a bet on the river if you don't have a lot of opponents and no overcards to your pair have fallen. If they check to you again on the river after you've checked the turn, you should bet.

One final thought about this situation: many players would never raise with an eight on the flop — they would wait until the turn to raise. If that's the sort of player you're up against and he raises on the flop, then you can treat your queens as the best hand and keep betting.

Obviously, if the board is paired *over* your pocket pair, you can fold at the first opportunity. In this case, you might not win even if you catch your miracle card.

The situation is similar if you pair one of your cards, and the other two cards are a pair. For instance, you have A♦-J♣ and the flop comes J♠-6♥-6♦. You can play it as you would the first example. However, note that if you catch your miracle card (another jack), you will now terrify somebody with a six, and he will just check and call, if that. Furthermore, you have to split the pot with the case jack if somebody has it. Therefore, this hand is even weaker than the first example and should be treated as such.

A bluffing opportunity

Note that the situation is not hopeless. In a nine-person game, if you see two eights on the flop and you don't have one, there is a 40% chance that nobody at the table was dealt an eight. Furthermore, somebody may have folded an eight (watch for signs that somebody is upset about dropping before the flop). This is one of the few situations in a low-limit game where you can try a pure bluff. If nobody has an eight, you might win the pot right there with a bet, even if you have nothing.

---

[2]This is an example of the concept we discussed earlier — using the flop to get information so you do the right thing on later, more expensive, bets.

Playing When You Flop Trips

Low-limit hold'em players lose a lot of money by not playing trips fast enough.

Y ou flop trips very infrequently: about 11% of the time when you hold a pocket pair, and less than 2% of the time when you hold two cards of different rank. However, you will often make a lot of money when you get these hands.

When you flop a set

A "set" is three of a kind when you have two of the rank in your hand and a third one is on the board. This is an extremely powerful hand (partially because it is so well hidden), and many players are tempted to play it slowly so they can extract the most money from their opponents. This brings us to the sentence at the beginning of the chapter: almost all the time, you do better by playing your set fast, putting in as many bets and raises as possible. This is particularly true in low-limit hold'em because you will not scare players out of the pot the way you would in higher limit games. For instance, if you get somebody opposite you at the table with two pair, you will often cap the betting between you, making it terribly expensive for straight and flush draws. In low-limit games, you may trap in players who have only two overcards and are drawing dead.

However, if you play the hand slowly, you are giving hands such as inside straight draws a better chance to beat you. For instance, suppose you have

And the flop comes

You have flopped the absolute nuts. However, if a club or any 3, 5, 6, 8, T, or J comes on the turn, you may no longer be in front (you are a 3.4:1 dog to make a full house or quads on the river). Thus, in most cases, you want to get lots of money in the pot right now. You are an almost 3:1 favorite over an open-end straight draw, and you will still win 60% of the pots against *both* an open-end straight draw and a club flush draw in this situation. When your opponents put money in the pot, you are getting an enormous return on your investment.

Conversely, if you let them in cheaply, they are getting much better odds on their draws, making those draws either less of a mistake, or even correct. If that is the case, you are losing money. For instance, if there is a bet in front of you and you flat call, a player with

is getting correct implied odds to call (trying to catch an eight) if there were about six bets in the pot before the flop. However, if you raise the original bettor, a person who calls with an inside straight draw (even to the nuts) is making a mistake.

Often you will hear players say, "There was no point in betting (or raising) — he would have called with his flush draw anyway." The latter half of this statement is true, but misleading. A player who calls your bets or raises when he has flopped four to a flush is not making a mistake. However, if you check and let him draw at his flush for free, you are giving him *infinite* odds on his draw (pot size: 0), which is far better for him than your charging him a bet for his draw. The situation is similar, but not quite as bad, if you call a bet rather than raising.

Note that typically you are *both* doing the correct thing. If there are players in the pot other than you and the flush draw, they are subsidizing both of you. Since you have the best hand, you have the most equity in the pot and benefit from every dollar that goes in. Your opponent with the flush draw is getting the correct pot odds (2:1) to draw. Everybody else is probably making a serious mistake, as it's likely they're drawing dead or near dead.

Remember, if you raise on the flop with your set, and half as many people call as would have called a single bet, you have gotten the same amount of money in the pot but you're competing with half as many opponents. Slowplaying is intended to let lesser hands catch up to a monster — and your set is not a monster (yet).

Exceptions

There are two cases in which you might want to slow down after you've flopped a set:

1. You are very sure you have the best hand and are willing to risk giving your opponents a cheap card in hopes of building a bigger pot.

2. You're concerned that you may not have the best hand.

Let's consider the first case. Suppose you have a pair of red sevens, and the flop comes

Especially if you are in late position, you may want to just call if there is a bet in front of you, or even check if there hasn't been a bet. You are taking a risk (note that a 4, 5, 6, or ace could give somebody a straight), but it may be worth it. With this flop, you won't get much action from many hands. However, if a card like the 3♠ comes on the turn, maybe you can catch an opponent (or two) with a three, and even get some spade flush draws interested. Of course, you're happy for this to happen because it's virtually impossible for anybody to catch up with you if another three does fall. If something like the 8♦ comes, you may now have a problem because somebody could have picked up a very big draw. However, you can now bet or raise on the turn and make it a questionable play for those draws to stay in.

Note that this is the exceptional case. If the flop contains any two cards of the same suit, you are probably better off playing fast. You simply cannot afford to give a possible flush draw a cheap card.

Another case in which you can slow down is when your opponent shows aggression on the flop. Suppose you are in the situation above (you have pocket sevens and flop top set) in early position. You bet out and are raised by a player in late position. You can choose to re-raise on the flop, or wait until the turn. If you go with the latter plan, your intent on the turn should be to trap as many people as possible for as many bets as possible. If most of the players are between you and the raiser, bet out. If he raises, re-raise. If the raiser is immediately behind you, then go for the check-raise, hoping players behind him will call his bet, and then you get to raise them.

Now consider the other case — what if you're afraid you're up against a bigger hand? This is an unusual scenario. However, suppose you have a pair of red nines and get a flop like

Even now, you probably want to start out playing fairly fast. There is a chance you're up against a made straight or a flush. There's even a chance you're drawing dead to a straight flush.[1] However, you don't want to give a single ten or spade a free card, so you have to grit your teeth and bet or raise. If you are re-raised, you can back off (call) to see how the turn and river cards look. Note that with a pair of red aces, you would play this hand very fast on the flop, but you'd be prepared to drop them if a lot of players were betting and raising. With a set, you can't get away so easily. You have to see this hand to the end, so you may want to ease up and see what the turn and river cards bring. Now if the board pairs, you *hope* somebody made a straight and somebody else made a flush, because you beat them both and they'll likely call a raise on the river.

If the pot has gotten big on the flop (i.e. there's been a raise or two and/or many players in the hand) don't even think about slowplaying; get your raises in immediately.

A final thought about sets — if you *never* folded after flopping a set, you probably wouldn't be making much of a mistake. Play them fast, and plan to go to the river with them.

---

[1] There is also a saying that if you get a set beaten and don't lose a lot of chips, you didn't play it right. This is somewhat simplistic, but emphasizes the importance of playing aggressively with a hand this strong.

When you flop trips (with a pair on the board)

You have to play this hand much more delicately than you do a flopped set. With a pair on the board, everybody will be nervous about where the other two of that rank are. If another player is aggressive, you may be looking at the fourth card of that rank, a hand that can beat trips, a bluff, or a hand that looks good but isn't as good as yours. Let's consider an example. You have

in late position with four callers in front of you and the flop comes

If somebody bets here, raise. The pot has gotten fairly large (especially if the bettor is early and there are callers in between), and your hand isn't strong enough to slow-play. If somebody re-raises you, there's a reasonable chance that he has the last eight. Now you back off and call any bets.

A lot of players will raise with a queen in this situation, but with an eight they will wait to raise on the turn.[2] Therefore, if you bet and somebody raises, it doesn't prove that he has the case eight. This is a good time to try for a check-raise on the turn, as your

---

[2]Another reason for you to raise on the flop with a third eight. You're getting more money in the pot, and may actually be persuading your opponents that you *don't* have the eight.

opponent with a queen (or less) may bet the turn. Again, figure out what will trap the most players for the most bets and do that.

If you have a very strong kicker with your trips, you want to play it even faster. In the case above, if you have A♦-8♦ instead of 8♦-7♦, you can put in four or five bets. This severely punishes somebody who has the case eight but no kicker. It also puts the most possible pressure on straight and flush draws. Sometimes the person with the smaller kicker will get lucky and pair his kicker to make a full house — you simply take that chance. If you're pretty sure you have the best kicker with the trips, play the hand very strongly.

In looser hold'em games, you will almost assuredly get to the river with trips. In the above case, only another queen falling would make you inclined to drop. Even then, you would have to be quite sure there was a third queen somewhere because the pot would probably be enormous. Of course, if the board is terribly scary for you (for instance, you have T♠-8♠ and the board is showing 8♦-8♣-7♦-6♣-5♦) and there is a lot of action, save your money and get out. Learning when to fold strong hands takes years of experience and practice. It is one of the skills you must develop to move to higher limits and tougher games.

Playing When You Flop a Straight or Flush Draw

S traight and flush draws are much stronger hands in low-limit games than they are in bigger limits. The main reasons for this are:

1. As we have discussed previously, you will usually have many opponents in the pot with you. Their presence makes the straight and flush draws correct in cases that would not be right if you had fewer opponents. In short, you are getting the necessary pot odds.

2. You will get paid off more often when you do make your hand — the pots will be (relatively) bigger than they are in more expensive games, and your opponents are more inclined to call. In short, you are getting better implied odds.

3. Because there are typically so many players in a hand, the average winning hand will be closer to the best *possible* hand (i.e., the nuts) than it is in a tighter game. The best possible hand for any given board is rarely less than a straight, so you will need these more powerful hands more frequently to win a pot.

Since you are drawing, you want many players to stay in the pot with you (just as you do with drawing hands before the flop). In fact, you are often in a situation where you can bet or raise your draws for value. "For value" means that with enough callers, you show a profit on bets you make, even though you're still drawing. Thus, your goal is to get as many players as possible to put in as many bets as possible.

Big draws

Consider this example.[1] You are in late position with

There are five callers in front of you, you call, the button raises, and everybody calls. Now the flop comes

Note that there are *fifteen* bets in the pot already. If it's checked to you, you should bet. Even if the pre-flop raiser raises now, at least a few of the people in front will call the raise. You are slightly less than a 2:1 underdog to make your flush, so you are making money if you can get at least three other people in the pot with you. You need to get slightly better than the exact odds since you could make the flush but have it beaten by a full house.

In low-limit games, you will often have four or more opponents with you on the flop. In that case, just try to maximize the number of bets that go in. If four bets are going into the pot for every bet you put in, you are getting much the best of it. Of course, this assumes that you're drawing at the nut flush or straight. If you aren't, you need to consider the possibility that your hand won't be good if you make it. With a draw to less than the nuts, you can

---

[1]For much of this chapter you can consider straight and flush draws interchangeably. A four-flush is a 1.9:1 underdog to make a flush by the river. The open-ended straight draw is a 2.2:1 underdog. These are close enough to consider equivalent for now.

still call the bets and raises, but you probably shouldn't be putting them in yourself.

Raising with a draw in late position can also have the desirable side effect of getting you a free card on the turn should you need one. Suppose you have A♠-J♠ on the button and there were three calls in front of you pre-flop. You call, as do both blinds, and the flop comes as above (Q♠-4♠-T♥). You have an extremely strong hand — any king or spade (with the minor exception of the T♠) gives you the nuts. An ace may give you the best hand as well. If there is a bet and a couple of calls, you should raise as much as 90%-95% of the time. You probably don't have the best hand right now — somebody almost surely has a queen — but you are getting excellent odds for your draw (you will make either the straight or the flush 45% of the time). Now if you make your hand on the turn, you can bet. If the turn misses you, you check and get a free river card. You may also get people betting into you on the river after you've checked the turn. Of course, if you make your hand on the river, you get to raise them.

Suppose you are in late position, and call with

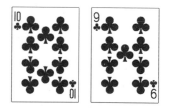

after four other players have called. Now the flop comes

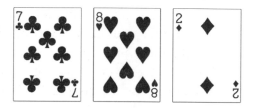

The first player bets, two people call, and you (correctly) raise with the open-end straight draw. But now the original bettor makes it three bets. If there is a caller or two between you, and *particularly* if your cardroom permits only three raises, go ahead and cap it. Since you are getting 2:1 or 3:1 on the bets you put in, you're not taking the worst of it by re-raising. Furthermore, because you've capped the betting in late position, the original bettor doesn't know what you have. For all he can tell, you have pocket eights and are just raising with the best hand. Now there is a very good chance that he'll check to you on the turn, giving you the free card if necessary.

Note that if the turn is a club, you pick up a flush draw as well. In that case, you may have as many as 15 (or more) outs - you can bet the turn for value.

A final benefit of this play: by building a huge pot on the flop, you encourage your opponents to call your bets if you make your hand.

You can also check-raise with a draw if you're sure that people between you and the bettor will call (or if they've already called one bet). Remember, you don't want to shut people out of the hand now. Suppose you are in the situation we described previously (you have A♠-J♠; flop is Q♠-4♠-T♥) but are in early position. You check, there is a bet immediately to your left and three callers. Raise if you're pretty sure the bettor won't re-raise. Your problem with his re-raising is that he may scare out the callers to his left, and you don't want that. If he just calls, the original callers will call your single raise.

Of course, check-raising in early position puts you in an awkward situation on the turn. If a blank hits, you *have* to check since it's virtually impossible you will win the hand by betting, and you probably won't get the four callers you need to make a bet for value correct (if the turn misses you, you are a 4:1 underdog to make your flush on the river). Your check on the turn shows weakness, and you may be forced to call a bet.

Remember, if you're going to check-raise with a draw, do it with a draw to the nuts.[2]

Double gutshot straight draws

You need to recognize these because they are effectively open-end straight draws made up of two inside straight draws. Suppose you have

and the flop comes

If you don't look closely, you may miss the fact that *either* a king or a nine gives you the nuts. Play this hand the way you would an open-end straight draw. In bigger games you'll learn that these hands are especially valuable for their deceptive qualities. At lower-limits, few if any of your opponents will be trying to work the hand backwards to see what you have.

Another example: you have 7♠-5♠ in the big blind, and the flop comes 9♣-6♥-3♠. Any eight or four gives you a straight. However, note that if an eight comes, you don't have the nut straight (check this and be sure you know what *is* the nuts).

---

[2]In his seminal work, *Hold'em Poker*, David Sklansky wrote, "Never check-raise on the flop with a come hand if a pair shows." This is as good advice now as it was when I first read it many years ago, but at the time my ignorance of poker terminology made the sentence almost indecipherable to me.

Weaker draws

The best draw worth mentioning here is the inside straight draw. Contrary to the advice passed down through innumerable generations of American men ("And son, don't *ever* draw to an inside straight..."), it is often correct in low-limit hold'em to do just that. You are an 11:1 underdog to catch your card on the turn, but you can count on winning some big bets if you do (implied odds again). Therefore, you can call a bet on the flop if you're getting about 7:1 odds, assuming that you are drawing at the nuts. For instance, if the flop is two-suited, you must be getting substantially better odds to draw at the inside straight because you might make your straight at the same time somebody makes a flush.

It is even better if you have two overcards to the flop. For instance, suppose you have J♦-T♦ and the flop comes 8♣-7♥-2♠. Now a nine gives you the nuts, and either a jack or ten may give you the best hand. This is the best possible situation in which to draw at a "gutshot" straight.

You will occasionally see players drawing at the low (aptly called the "ignorant") end of an inside straight (for example, they have 6♥-5♥, the flop comes 8♣-9♦-A♠, and they call a bet trying to catch a seven). Unless you are getting enormous pot odds — say 20:1 or better — don't do this.

Usually if there's a raise on the flop and you would have to call two bets cold, you are not getting correct odds to draw at an inside straight. If you call a single bet and there's a raise behind you, then you can call. However, you would rather see this situation coming and not call the first bet. You can sometimes call on the turn with an inside straight draw, but remember you're an 11:1 underdog to make your straight. This is an excellent example of why you need to keep track of the number of bets in the pot — were there 22 small bets in the pot before you had to call on the turn? If so, then you can call with your inside straight draw.

Sometimes the combination of a couple of draws will make it correct for you to call a bet on the flop. For instance, suppose you have

and the flop comes

You have two overcards to the flop, so a king or queen will probably give you the best hand. Furthermore, you can catch two running spades to make a big flush. You are a 2.8:1 underdog against somebody with an eight, so if you can get 5:1 or 6:1 odds (which is almost always), it's worth a call. You need better than 2.8:1 odds because some of your outs involve catching a spade on the turn and then making your flush on the river. In that case you may have to call a bet on the turn while you're still drawing. If you don't catch top pair on the turn or pick up your flush draw, you should fold.

Straight draws vs. flush draws

We said at the beginning of this chapter that you could treat straight and flush draws similarly because the odds against your making them were similar. However, there are some differences you need to understand.

If you flop a straight draw when the flop is two-suited, you must consider the chance that making your straight with the third card of a suit will do you no good. In effect, you have only six outs instead of eight. Even if your straight *is* good when the third of the suit hits, you won't get as much value for it because you can't play as aggressively. Furthermore, opponents you can beat will be less inclined to call because either a straight *or* flush beats them. If a flush draw is possible, you have to be more tactful in handling your straight draw. Continuing this thought, do *not* draw at a straight if there are three of the same suit on the board. You will see other players do it, but throw away a straight draw without a second thought if a flush could be made already. In the long run, this will save you a lot of money.

When the board is paired

You must proceed much more carefully when you flop draws with the board paired — you may be drawing dead, or almost dead. For instance, if you have J♣-T♣ and the flop comes 8♦-8♠-9♥, you have an open end straight draw. However, if an opponent has 8♥-7♥, your straight draw is actually an inside straight draw because only a queen is good. A seven falling is *terrible* because it makes your straight but gives your opponent a full house.

In that case, you have to be getting better pot odds to proceed. Don't raise with draws in that case — you're not drawing to the nuts. Don't draw at an inside straight at all; the implied odds are simply not there.

If the flop is a single suit

If the flop is all one suit, you can continue if you have the nut or second nut flush draw. Anything else, there's too much of a chance that you're drawing dead. Since you may be up against a completed flush already (which reduces your chances of making your flush), don't raise for value — although if you have position, think about raising for a free card and then checking on the turn if you don't make your flush.

Final thought on draws

One of the biggest differences between low-limit hold'em and the bigger games is the number of opportunities to bet draws for value. By doing this correctly, you can win a handful of extra bets during a session and yet be perceived as somebody who "gambles." That is, you don't want your opponents to think you play only quality cards and good draws. If they realize that, they won't pay you off when you make big hands. Putting a lot of bets into the pot with a draw is often viewed as gambling — going against the odds just for the excitement of the draw. However, with enough opponents, you're doing the mathematically correct thing while your opponents see you playing loose and wild. This is an extraordinarily powerful combination.

Playing When You Flop a Complete Hand

Every once in a great while, you will be fortunate enough to flop a "complete" hand — straight or better.

When you flop a straight

This is the weakest of the complete hands, and is vulnerable to the most draws. Therefore, you want to play a flopped straight fast. Also, any time you flop a complete hand, your opponents will be slow to give you credit for it — you may get almost unlimited raises from two pair or a set. Consider the following example: you have

in late position. There are three calls in front of you; the button and both blinds call. Now the flop comes

There is a bet and two calls in front of you. Many players would just call in this situation — that's a *mistake* — you should definitely raise. There are already nine bets in the pot, and there are many cards you don't want to see on the turn. If any heart or five through nine falls on the turn, you no longer have the nuts. Furthermore, if somebody has flopped a set or two pair, he may choose to slow play it (which is also a mistake, though in this case it's to his benefit). Your raise may cause him to re-raise immediately and you re-raise again. Note that this puts enormous pressure on heart draws and hands like T♦-8♦, which is important. Of course, playing this fast on the flop will knock out some players who have little or no chance to beat you. You're better off paying that price and forcing draws to pay a premium.

If you flop an ace high straight and there are no flush draws that worry you, you can slow down a little bit. If you have A♠-Q♠ and the flop is K♥-J♦-T♠, it's OK to check and call or just flat call a bet. However, if a lot of action breaks out, you should take off the gloves and start raising yourself — if somebody has two pair or a set, you want to punish them now while you know you have the nuts. By playing slowly, you run the risk of a card such as the Q♣ falling (in which case you have to split the pot with any ace) or a very scary card like the J♥ (which makes full houses possible and may give somebody a heart flush draw). The more players you have against you, the more inclined you should be to play your straight fast.

If you flop the non-nut straight (you have 8♦-7♦ and the flop comes J♠-9♦-T♣), it's even more important to play fast. If an eight, queen, or king comes, you have essentially nothing, so you have to start swinging immediately. Even trying to check-raise is probably a mistake. Go ahead and bet, hoping you get raised so you can re-raise. If somebody has KQ (or Q8), you are going to lose some chips — you can't give up this hand unless a couple of very scary cards hit.

When you flop a flush

This is another situation where many players make a serious mistake by not playing fast enough. If you flop anything but the nut flush, you *must* bet or raise to charge higher flush draws dearly. Suppose you have

in middle position, you call along with four others, the big blind raises, and you all call. Now the flop comes

and the big blind bets out. Slowplaying is out of the question here. The pot is so big you'd be happy to win the whole thing right here (but that isn't going to happen). Anybody with the A♦ or K♦ is going to call (which is correct for them). Raise immediately. If somebody makes it three bets, you can flat call, but you still need to bet again on the turn if a blank comes — you don't dare give a single bigger diamond a free card. Again, if somebody has flopped a bigger flush than you, you will lose some money. However, far more frequently you will have the best hand — but you must play it fast.

If a fourth diamond comes, you are now in a check and call situation, especially if anybody called your raise cold on the flop. There is still some chance you have the best hand, but you don't want to call a raise with it. If a fourth of your suit comes and you have a lower flush (say eight or nine high), you may have to give it up. The fact that you most likely were well in front on the flop means nothing — throw your six card flush away if there is significant action.

If you flop the nut flush, you can wait until the turn to raise or check-raise. However, as we discussed with the straight, if a raising war breaks out on the flop, you should start raising as well. If the board pairs, then don't check-raise — you might be giving a full house a chance to make it three big bets. Bet out immediately and hope you are called but not raised. If you are raised, you should call. Only if the board pairs twice should you be willing to abandon the nut flush.

When you flop a full house

With a pocket pair, you will flop a full house a little more than 1% of the time; with two cards of different rank, about 0.1% of the time (one out of a thousand hands). In general, your only concern at this point is how to extract the most money from the hand — your chances of being beaten are minuscule.

With pocket pairs, you can flop a full house in two different ways: one of your rank plus a pair, or trips on the board. Of course, you prefer the former way — in the latter case there's always the danger that somebody has the fourth one. First, let's consider the "set+pair" scenario. Suppose you have

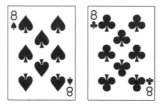

in middle position with six callers. Now the flop comes

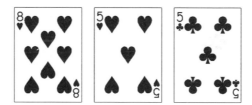

This is an excellent situation for you. Of course, you hope that the other two fives are active[1] and that there is a flush draw around as well. Your hand is altogether strong enough to slow play, but you may not want to do that. If one or two players have fives, you want them to start betting and raising immediately, so you might bet or raise once to get things going. However, you don't want to scare anybody at this point. Let other people do the raising on the flop. If you're lucky, the turn will complete the

---

[1]In different hands.

flush, and two other people will do all the raising for you while you are just along for the ride. Things will probably slow down on the river, and that's when you can get in your raise(s).

If no flush or straight draw is possible on the flop, you should slow down a lot, hoping the turn will give some people big draws (that are probably dead). However, once the turn comes, you should start betting and raising. A person with a flush draw will only complete it one out of five times on the river. By raising on the turn, you get these people to call, trying to make their flushes and straights. You're delighted if they make them on the river, but usually they don't, so you need to collect from them on the turn.

The situation is somewhat different if your set is the lower of the two ranks on the board. Suppose you have those same black eights, but the flop is

 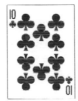 

This is a wonderful flop for you, but not quite as good as the first one. Unlike the first case, there is a small, but important chance you will get out drawn. Furthermore, you will usually have to pay off some pretty big raises when you are beaten. However, until almost guaranteed otherwise, you must play this as the best hand. This time, you can't wait to show aggression. Start betting and raising immediately on the flop — with the negligible exceptions of TT or T8, you are winning for now. Don't hesitate to cap the betting on the flop given the opportunity. The same is true on the turn — play the hand strongly. Be willing to put in a third bet on the turn, and only get nervous if somebody puts in a fourth bet. Sometimes you lose to a bigger full house with this hand, but worrying about that very much is seeing monsters under the bed. Play it for the best hand, and just be alert for the small possibility that one of those monsters is real.

If the board pairs (such as two running sixes), you will probably have to fold. Fortunately, this doesn't happen very often, but if you have been getting a lot of action on the turn, and then the turn card pairs, your full house is almost worthless. Furthermore, you're going to get caught in a raising war if both tens are active. Give up and get out.

If the flop is all one rank when you have a pocket pair (.24% of the time), you have an awkward situation. If you have a big pair (tens or higher), you probably have to stay with it as long as no overcards fall. If an overcard to your pair hits, you are beaten by a single one of those as well as the fourth card of the flopped rank; now you can get out if there's a lot of action. If you have a big pair you should bet the flop to avoid giving bigger cards a free card. Also, in this situation, almost anybody who has flopped the quads is going to slow-play. Use bets and raises on the flop to figure out who is willing to stick around. For instance, watch out for a player who calls a raise cold on the flop — proceed carefully. Plan to check and call on the turn and river — somebody with quads will probably wait for big bets to raise.

If you hold two cards of different rank and flop a full house, the situation is similar to flopping top set with a smaller pair. Suppose you hold and call in middle position after two other callers. Now there is a caller behind you, a raise, and two cold calls. Everybody else calls. The flop comes

You've got the nuts, and the chance of your being out drawn at this point is almost nil. Unfortunately, it's unlikely that you're going to get much action from anybody. If somebody has the case jack, he'll play with you — other than that you have to hope that there are some straight and flush draws out. You might as well start betting with this hand — hope that the last jack is, in fact, active, and that player starts raising. Many players will stay in with their draws here even though they're drawing dead.

When you flop quads or a straight flush

This happens so infrequently it's hardly worth mentioning. With the quads, you've crippled the deck (i.e., it's unlikely anybody else has a hand that they like much). In a higher limit game, you might want to slow down and relieve the fears of your opponents about who had made trips. In a low-limit game, it doesn't matter much. Check once on the flop to see what people do, but if any betting and raising happens, get in and raise too.

With the straight flush, you probably want to play fairly fast because if somebody has the ace high flush, he may put in a lot of bets before he figures out he's beaten (assuming the board isn't paired). Your hand is very well hidden and you will get a lot of action from worse hands. Therefore, there's no point in slow-playing even though there's (essentially) no danger of your being out drawn.

Summary — flopping a complete hand

Once again we see that even when you flop a huge hand, you rarely want to slow play it in a low-limit game. Players will not give you credit for the hand that you have and will happily raise even though they may be drawing dead. Give them plenty of opportunities to do this by playing your big hands fast.

Playing When You Flop Two Overcards

Overcards are cards higher than anything on the board. Let's consider an example. You have

and the flop comes

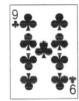 

You have two overcards — can you call a bet? Can you bet? Many poker experts say that you can bet or call a bet in this situation. However, it takes a lot of experience and knowledge to know when you can play with just overcards. A bet with two overcards is usually a semi-bluff (you're hoping to win the pot right there, but have chances of improving to the best hand). Most low-limit games are sufficiently loose and passive that a semi-bluff won't work, so betting is probably not correct.

We believe you are not losing much by folding in this situation if there's a bet ahead of you. If it's checked to you, take a free card and hope you turn top pair. In the situation above, if a queen or king falls on the turn, you probably have the best hand and can bet (or even raise).

Expert players are able to make some money with two overcards, but you are not giving up much by dropping them unless you have other possibilities (which we discuss below). Misplaying those overcards once or twice will cost you more than you could make by playing them correctly a dozen times.

The problem with overcards is that you can win a little or lose a lot. Most of the time, you'll have to throw them away on the turn because they don't improve. Therefore, to make a profit with them, you must play aggressively when they do hit on the turn. If you pick the wrong time to do this, you may be raising with the worst hand. This is an area where you can improve your results by limiting your mistakes. Until you have a lot of hold'em under your belt and understand your opponents well, you can best limit your mistakes by staying out of these situations.

When you can play overcards

There *are* some situations in which you can call a bet with overcards:

Backdoor flush or straight possibilities. For instance, you have A♠-T♠ and the flop comes 9♥-6♠-2♣. Now you can call a bet since an ace or ten may give you the best hand, and another spade on the turn gives you the nut flush draw. If you're hoping to make a backdoor straight, the turn should possibly give you an open end draw to the nuts. For instance, you have Q♣-J♣ and the flop comes 9♥-4♠-3♦. Again, you could make top pair on the turn, and a ten will give you a draw to two different nut straights.

The higher your cards, the better, so if you do make the top pair on the turn, you will have fewer chances for an overcard to *your* top pair falling on the river.

A-K overcards on the flop

AK (often called "Big Slick") is one of the most difficult hands to play if it "misses" the flop. You will either make top pair or two overcards with it, so you often find yourself wanting to continue with it, almost regardless of the flop. Do not fall victim to this trap. If you're going to call with two overcards, AK is the hand with which to do it, but choose your places carefully. Look for situations where you're virtually certain that hitting your pair will be good, you have backdoor draws, or suspect that an opponent is betting a draw. Furthermore, it is almost *never* correct to call a bet on the turn with an unpaired AK, unless you've picked up some other draw.

Once in a great while, you can raise with AK when it doesn't pair on the flop, particularly if you suspect that the bettor doesn't have a good hand. On rare occasions, this may cause the bettor to fold immediately, or at least get you a free turn card. If you are re-raised, or the bettor calls and then bets the turn, you are done with the hand. Realize that this is a deceptive play, and such plays have limited use in most low-limit games.

Many players can not give up AK until the river fails to pair them; a classic tip-off is when somebody raises pre-flop and then passively calls a bet on the flop. If you detect such behavior, be prepared to bet hands that you might otherwise check on the turn; don't give the two overcards a free chance to beat you.

A word of warning

In tighter games, you can use the flop to decide the chances that you're up against two pair already. However, in a no fold'em hold'em game, many players are capable of showing you *any* two cards. For instance, in a tighter hold'em game you'd be more inclined to play overcards with a flop of T-5-2 since it would be unlikely somebody already had two pair. In lower limit games, you will see people win big pots with T5. This is another reason why it's a marginal play to continue with just overcards in low-limit hold'em games.

You will routinely see your opponents continue playing (even calling a raise cold) with two overcards to the flop. You will also occasionally be sitting on the sidelines watching when your overcards would have made the best hand. Have faith, and throw them away the next time, too. For low-limit hold'em players, flopping two overcards is a marginal case of our next topic: what to do when the flop misses you completely.

Playing When the Flop Misses You

In completing our discussion of how to play on the flop, we need to remind you that this, unfortunately, will be the most frequent result of the flop: you get a very small piece of it, or less.

You'll flop second or bottom pair with no overcards. Three to a flush or straight and nothing else. One overcard.

Your opponents will routinely call a bet in this situation, hoping to pick up a little more on the turn. This is where decisive action can save you a lot of money:

Fold and be done with it.

We have discussed essentially every case in which you can play beyond the flop. Every other time, your pre-flop investment is gone. Forget about it. Watch the rest of the hand. See how your opponents play, figure out what you would do in a similar situation. Get up and stretch, drink a glass of water. However, do not just throw in a loose call on the flop to see what happens next. This discipline alone will take you a long way toward becoming a winning hold'em player.

Bluffing on the flop

Suppose the flop misses you completely, but it looks very ragged and you think it might have missed everybody else too. Is this a good time to bluff? In a bigger limit game, the answer might well be yes. In a low-limit hold'em game, you're probably wasting your money. We will go into more detail about bluffing in a later chapter, but for now, consider what we said above. Many of your opponents don't think twice about calling a bet on the flop — they just throw the chips in. Against that kind of opposition, a bluff is simply not profitable. It makes many more *value* bets profitable (i.e., when you have a good or great hand), but trying to represent a hand you don't have won't work often enough to be worth it.

Free Cards and the Importance of Position

A s you advance in your poker career, you will develop an arsenal of subtle plays and tricks to use on your opponents. Unfortunately, you won't be able to practice them much in low-limit hold'em games — they simply won't work. However, there is one very powerful play that works quite well in low-limit games — the *free card*.

The free card play is simply raising in late position with a hand that's not likely to be the best at the moment. Your intent is to freeze up bettors in front of you on the next card, giving you the option of betting, or checking and seeing the following card for free. In the $3-$6 game, you've put in an extra $3 bet so you don't have to call $6 on the turn. Every time this play works for you, *it saves you $3*.

A classic example

You are on the button with

and are the fifth caller. Then the little blind raises and everybody calls. Now the flop comes

There is a bet and two callers in front of you. With 14 bets in the pot, you have an easy call. If the turn is an eight, you have the nuts. A jack or ten may give you the best hand, and if a diamond

falls, you pick up a flush draw. If you raise (instead of calling), the players in front of you will probably check on the turn. Of course, if you get lucky and turn the straight or top pair, you bet. Otherwise, you check and see the river card for free. This play is almost always successful in passive low-limit games and has enormous value to you.

Other good opportunities to use the free card play:

* Second pair with an overcard kicker and perhaps a backdoor straight or flush draw. Suppose you have A♣-T♣ in late position and the flop comes T♥-Q♣-2♥. If there is a bet in front of you and you are in last position or (particularly) feel that a raise will knock out any player(s) behind you, seriously consider raising. While it's likely you're up against a queen, it's worth a shot to catch a ten, ace, or backdoor flush draw.[1]

* Flush draw in late position when there's a bet in front. You'd rather not call a bet on the turn if you don't make your flush; raise on the flop, hoping to make the original bettor check on the turn. You probably aren't giving up a raise if you make your flush on the turn. Many players will freeze up at the sight of a third suited card and check anyway.

  Raising here also has some deceptive value. Your opponents may assume that you had top pair or something when you raised on the flop (which you easily could have). Now when the flush card hits, they may bet at you, representing the flush. Of course, your raise on the turn shows them they're mistaken.

The importance of position

You see that to make the free card play, you generally must be in late position, preferably last to act. This points out yet another reason why you have to pay such close attention to your position.

---

[1]Depending on the pot size and other factors, you may need to call a bet on the river with your second pair and ace kicker.

Many hands that will simply not pay up front will make money for you in late position because you can use the free card play.

An added benefit of the "free card" raise may be to knock out players between you and the button. If there is one player behind you and you think your raise on the flop will knock him out, that's all the more reason to raise. "Buying the button" is an important tactic in making the hand go the way you want.

Defending against the free card

Unfortunately, you have to take your turn in the early and middle positions. Sometimes you will bet on the flop and get raised by a player in late position. If you think he's capable of trying to get a free card, what should you do? If you believe you have the best hand, re-raise immediately, or call and then bet on the turn. As you can see, this is an awkward situation since he may have you beaten, and you're just giving him more chances to raise. However, you should be aware of the possibility that somebody is trying to get a free card, and defend against that.

The difficulty of defending against the free card shows both how powerful a play it is and the importance of having good position. Remember that when you're thinking about playing marginal hands in early position before the flop.

Confrontations on the Flop

Warning: you will have to make full use of your experience and judgment in situations such as we describe below. Treat the following as guidelines, not rules.

Ideally, if you're going to play a hand after the flop, you want to take control of it. You should be doing the raising (unless of course you've flopped a monster), and generally making other players do what you want.

Dealing with a maniac

With weak loose players (calling stations), you can usually accomplish this. However, against a maniac, it's often impossible. He will happily re-raise you with a draw, any pair, or just on a bluff. You will find that a maniac is often being controlled by his ego — he wants to put in the last raise, or bluff you out of a pot with nothing. When you get into a situation like this, it's often best to bend and let him take control. Especially if you have position, you can afford to do this. Suppose you have

and raise after four players call. The flop comes

Two players check and the third bets. You raise, the first two players drop. Now the original bettor re-raises, and the player between you drops. The bettor could have a queen with a smaller kicker, two pair, a set, or even just a draw. If your opponent is a tight and highly predictable player, you might actually be able to fold here, but that would be the exception. The board will have to get scarier before you can drop. In this situation, simply call your opponent's re-raise.

If the turn card is not a club and he checks, you should bet in case he's drawing at a club flush.[1] Many players will put in a lot of bets with a flush draw on the flop (although you know this is not correct heads-up), so his check on the turn may be a clue to that. If the turn is not a club and he continues to bet, call again[2]. If the turn is a club and he bets, you may have to drop. If he has a flush, you're drawing dead, and will have to call again on the river. Even if he doesn't have the flush, he's willing to bet into a possible flush, and that implies some more strength. If the flush card comes and he checks, just check along. That play may induce him to bluff at you on the river (you should call a bet on the river regardless of what falls). If he did have a better hand but not a flush, you saved a bet by checking on the turn (don't bother betting on the turn to represent the flush — you'll get called).

The situation is slightly different if you have to act first. Suppose the hand went the same way, but you check-raised on the flop, and the original bettor made it three bets, narrowing the field to just two of you. You now just check and call, following the same plan as above. If you check on the turn and he checks, too, don't bet on the river. We will discuss this later, but it's a situation where you're not likely to get called unless you're beaten. Also, by checking twice on the turn and river, you encourage your opponent to bluff at you on the river. Again, be prepared to call a bet on the river unless there's something like four to a straight or four clubs on the board.

---

[1] Often, he'll be trying to put some kind of play on you and will fold when you bet on the turn.

[2] Actually, a better play here may be to raise the turn, and plan to check the river unless you improve.

When you have a great hand

If you have the nuts, and it's not possible that somebody has the same hand but is drawing, put in a lot of bets (at least four or five) before stopping. For instance, if you have

and the flop comes

you can put five or six bets. However, if you had A♣-J♣ instead of A♦-J♣, your opponent could have the big straight *and* a diamond draw as well. If so, he's "free rolling" on you. Now you have to stop at about four bets and hope that no diamonds show up.

If you have a great hand but don't have the nuts, then you have to back off earlier. You're not going to fold the hand (even on the turn and river because the pot has gotten huge). However, you need to consider the possibility that you're beaten. Suppose you have

and the flop comes

If you get into a raising war with two or more opponents, don't be afraid to put in the last raise. However, if you are heads up, and your opponent keeps raising, at some point you have to worry about pocket jacks. After four or five bets, back off and then check and call through the river. If your opponent checks, bet. Note that many players will play JT or 55 as strongly as you would play JJ, so you may still be winning, but you don't want to put in too many raises without the nuts.

Now, suppose you have the guaranteed nuts. Perhaps you have A♠-T♠ and the flop is J♠-8♠-4♠. You get into a raising war with a single opponent and, for whatever reason, he keeps raising. Once you're *absolutely* sure you have the nuts (don't forget to check for a possible straight flush), how many raises should you put in? The best chance your opponent can have here is that he flopped a set. If so, he'll make a full house or better to beat your flush about a third of the time: you are a 2:1 favorite. Nevertheless, if he *does* get lucky and improve, you lose a lot of money. Thus, your decision here is somewhat personal. If you are willing to invest all your chips in a very positive situation (which this is), go ahead and raise until he stops raising or one of you is out of chips. If not, stop at whatever point you feel comfortable. If you still have the nuts on the turn, you can make the same decision again, knowing you're an almost 4:1 favorite. As we'll discuss later, if you have the nuts on the river, don't stop raising.

Play on the Turn

I n general, your play on the turn and river will be more straight-forward than that on the flop.

If you have the best hand

If you feel you have the best hand, continue to bet it, especially if you are concerned about draws. For instance, suppose you have

and raised on the flop, which was

Two players (including the original bettor) called your raise. If the next card is not a jack, an overcard, or a club, you should bet again. A player with a jack will probably call, and you cannot give overcards and flush draws a free card.

If a scary does fall, you have a more awkward situation. You can't be sure if that helped your opponents or not. Giving some-body with A♣-K♦ a free card when a small club falls is a terrible mistake, but you will have to do that sometimes. Try not to be paranoid about the nuts always being up against you; if you think you still have the best hand, go ahead and bet.

If you're not sure you have the best hand

If you are afraid you might not have the best hand, and you aren't too worried about free cards, then it's better to check. For instance, suppose you have

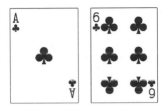

in late position, and the flop comes

It's checked to you, you bet, and two people call. Now the 8♣ comes on the turn and they both check again. You should normally check as well. There is a reasonable chance that one or both of your opponents has an ace with a better kicker. Furthermore, you're not as worried about giving a free card since overcards can't fall and there's no obvious draw. This is another situation where you'll probably have to call a bet on the river because your check on the turn showed weakness.

Drawing hands

Your hands that were marginal calls on the flop have now become clear in one direction or the other. Suppose you are in late position with

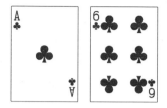

and six people take the flop for one bet. The flop is

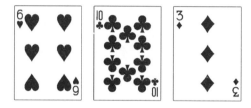

There is a bet and two calls and then you call. This is not an obvious call, but it's not a bad play either. However, the turn makes your decision easy: if you get a six or an ace, you raise; if you get a club, you call;[1] otherwise, you fold.

Most of your drawing hands will fall into similar situations by the turn. You can almost surely stay with strong flush and straight draws; it's likely you'll be getting the right odds to draw. However, if the board is paired, you have to be getting much better odds. If the third card of a suit hits on the turn, throw away your straight draw without a second thought.

Betting draws on the turn

There are times when it makes sense to bet a draw on the turn. Particularly if you're down to one or two opponents and you think there's any chance at all they might fold, it might be worth

---

[1]As mentioned before, in a tighter game, if you picked up a flush draw on the turn, a semi-bluff raise would be a powerful play.

betting. For instance, if you flopped a straight draw and turned a flush draw, or vice versa, you may have as many as 15 outs. If so, you're only about a 2:1 dog to win on the river, so you should probably bet. After all, you may win the pot on the turn, you may hit one of your outs, or your opponents may get tired of you betting all the time and fold on the river. A small pair with an overcard kicker and a flush draw often deserves a bet on the turn.

See if you can bet your draw on the turn for value. If not, ask yourself if there's a chance you might win the pot right there. If neither of those conditions holds, you should usually take a free card if you can get one.

Raising on the turn

You will probably not be doing as much raising on the turn as some of your opponents. They will often slow-play strong hands. As we discussed earlier, you are usually better off raising or check-raising on the flop. Once you have shown that strength early in the hand, your opponents will often check to you on the turn.

However, there will be times when you slow-play a hand, or improve your hand on the turn. If so, you should almost always start raising on the turn rather than wait for the river to raise. By raising on the turn, you are getting the most possible value for your strong hand, and forcing drawing hands to pay extra while there are cards yet to come. If you wait until the river, people who missed draws are not going to call a single bet, much less a raise.

Another time to raise on the turn is when you're going to call a bet on the river anyway, but could improve to a hand that is worth betting (or raising). For instance, suppose you have A♣–9♣ in late position, and get a flop of A♦–6♣–3♣. Now a five-way raising war breaks out. In spite of your marginal kicker, you're probably committed to calling a bet on the river even if you don't improve, because of the size of the pot. Particularly if the pot gets heads-up on the turn, you should raise, hoping to force your opponent into checking the river. Now if you improve (catching a nine or a club), you bet, otherwise you check. This way, you lose the same two big bets if you don't have the best hand, but win a third big bet if you improve. Also, this looks like "gambling" to your opponents, and mars your disciplined image.

If you are raised on the turn

This is a very difficult situation to handle correctly. A very common scenario is that you have top pair or an overpair that you bet on the turn, but you get raised. Your opponent is clearly telling you that he can beat top pair.

There are a few things to consider at this point. If your opponent is a very tight predictable player, you can be fairly sure that he has you beaten. If so, and you don't have the proper odds to draw, you can fold immediately. If the pot is large, you can call and see if you improve on the river (by making two pair or trips). If not, you can fold (your opponent will almost surely bet on the river).

You also need to think about the card that hit on the turn. Was it apt to have made the raiser two pair, or was he possibly slow-playing two pair that he had flopped? If the turn card was the second of a suit, is your opponent creative enough to raise when he picked up a flush draw?

Of course, there are some situations that are much easier to fold. If the turn was the third of a suit or an overcard to your pair, then it's much easier to fold without calling the raise. However, in many situations, you won't be so sure about what your opponent has, and the pot will be fairly large. In some of those cases, you will have to grit your teeth and call the raise and the (very probable) bet on the river. If you fold every time you are raised with an unimproved pair on the turn, you're giving up too much.

Calling raises in multi-way pots

In *most* situations, one pair (even a big pocket overpair to the board) is no longer in front if somebody is raising on the turn in a multi-way pot. This is a very difficult situation to handle correctly because the pot has often gotten quite large. But in general, if you have opponents raising and calling raises on the turn (or the river, for that matter), your top pair or overpair is probably not the best hand. Furthermore, you may be drawing extremely thin, or dead. Give serious consideration to giving up even powerful hands such as pocket aces and kings here.

Play on the River

When the river card is dealt, your play is fairly clear. There are, nevertheless, some important concepts to remember.

Betting good hands on the river

For instance, suppose you are drawing at a flush in early position and make your flush on the river. Many players will be tempted to check-raise in this situation. However, you should generally just bet immediately. If your opponent doesn't bet, you have cost yourself a bet. Furthermore, he may bet, but fold when you raise, so you win just one bet anyway.

The most obvious exception to this is when your opponent is a habitual bluffer. Then it might be worth checking, hoping that he'll bet whereas he wouldn't call your bet.

If you believe your opponent has a strong hand, you should not check-raise. If you bet, *he* might raise, giving you the opportunity to make it three bets.

Calling (or raising) big pots with marginal hands

Seven card stud players soon learn that they almost *have* to call a bet on the last card with any reasonable hand because the pot has become so large (after five betting rounds) that the price of making an incorrect fold is terribly high. Low-limit hold'em has a similar feature. Many players are normally contesting each pot, and they stay through most of the hand. Thus, by the end of the hand, the pot has a huge number of bets in it. In this situation, if your hand has even a tiny chance of winning, you must call.

Note, however, that occasionally you may be better off raising. Suppose the player in front of you bets and you believe he is bluffing, or has a weaker hand than yours. Furthermore, there are players to act behind you. In this case, you should seriously consider raising, hoping to force the players after you to fold. Now you just have to beat the original bettor rather than two or more opponents. This is a fairly strong play that you won't be able to use often, but if properly used, it can save you a large pot.

Multi-way pots

Sometimes when you have more than one opponent on the river, it's not obvious how to play a big hand. For instance, suppose you have made the nut flush on the river, a player bets into you, and there is a player behind you to act. Should you raise? With a single opponent, the answer is obvious — raise. However, in this case, you may want to call instead. If the original bettor is bluffing (or has great respect for you), you might win no further bets if both opponents fold for the raise whereas the player behind you might have called a single bet. Furthermore, if the player behind you has a smaller flush, he may raise, giving you an opportunity to make it three bets when the betting comes back around to you.

A similar situation happens when you think you have the best hand, but not the nuts. Now you'd rather get one bet from two people instead of two bets from one person. That way, if you're beaten, you lose one bet rather than two (or three). Suppose you make a flush on the river, but it's not the nut flush, or the board is paired. If there is a bet in front of you, you should normally call, hoping the player behind you will call as well. Raising will not force out a hand better than yours, but opens the door to either of your opponents re-raising, which you would prefer not happen.

Marginal hands lose much of their value in multi-way pots. If you have just one opponent, we've seen that you often have to call, even if it's a little questionable. However, if you have two or more opponents, your chances of having the best hand are greatly diminished. This is particularly true when you're last to act and already know that you have to beat two or more hands. In short, your hand must be very strong to overcall.

Raising forever with the best hand

Once in a while, you will get into a raising war on the river with a single opponent. You have the nuts, and yet he keeps raising. Once you're *sure* you have the nuts, how many raises should you put in? If you cannot be tied, then of course you should continue raising until your opponent stops or one of you is out of chips. If you could be tied, then you can probably stop at eight or nine bets. A good dealer will recognize the situation and keep your bets and those of your opponents separate, simplifying the subsequent pot split. If you suspect at *all* that your opponent is overplaying his hand, or doesn't recognize the true nuts, then happily raise until one of you is out of chips. Some players at your table may get upset about this if you do split the pot; ignore them. Even a slim chance that your opponent is wrong justifies unlimited raising.

If the nuts is on the board (e.g. J♥-K♦-T♦-A♠-Q♣), you might occasionally try a bet or raise to knock out oblivious opponents (the pot is split among all remaining players). However, don't take this play too far; very few players will fall for it.

Betting only when you want to be called

We have saved the most important concept in this chapter for last.[1] Just because you think you have the best hand on the end doesn't mean you should bet. You should only bet on the end if you'll have the best hand most of the time *when you're called*. For instance, suppose you have

---

[1]Here in the second edition, that's not quite true. This is the second most important concept, and it's the penultimate subsection. You can guess what's coming next.

and when the 3♠ falls on the river, the board looks like

You had bet on the flop and turn because you feared that your opponent was on a diamond flush draw. Now if you bet, one of two things will happen. If your opponent missed a flush draw he will throw his hand away. Otherwise, he had an ace with a better kicker (or better hand) and is checking and calling. In this situation, you will only be called if you are beaten, so you simply check your hand down.

Note that we are *not* talking about bluffing here. A bluff is a bet when you are fairly sure you don't have the best hand. In this case, you think you may well have the best hand, but you cannot bet it. Of course, if you think you can make some better hands fold, it may be to your advantage to bet. However, in low-limit hold'em games, this is rarely the case. If you think there's a fair chance that you have the best hand, then few of your opponents will be willing to fold a *better* hand.

In cases such as the above, you should be prepared to call a bet if you have to act first and check. Many of your opponents would continue betting your hand in this situation, and they assume you will too. Often when you check and call here, you will have the best hand.

A similar argument applies to raising on the river. If you are pretty sure you have the best hand, then of course you would raise. However, you must ask yourself if an opponent will call your raise with a hand worse than yours. If not, then you should not raise. Also, you have to consider the chance that you'll be re-raised. This further reduces the number of hands with which you should raise on the river.

This concept is extremely powerful and many poker players do not understand it. If you can spot these situations and play them correctly, you will save a lot of money over the course of your poker career.

You want to be called

This is the most important subsection in the chapter, if not the whole edition.

What I wrote in the previous paragraphs (about betting only when you want to be called) is absolutely true, and it's important to understand. But in the first edition, I didn't stress the following point enough:

Bet the river

Having read and followed the advice in this book and others like it, you are going to be playing premium hands. Your opponents will be playing premium hands and non-premium hands. In some cases they'll be playing junk. So most of the time when you get to the river and you've been betting for value the whole way, *keep betting*. This does not invalidate the dictum of only betting when you want to be called; the point is that you will constantly be called by worse hands.

The most profitable instance of this concept is when you're betting top pair with a big kicker, and your opponent is calling with top pair, smaller kicker.[2] Time after time, he will call, look at your cards, and say, "Good kicker" as he throws his hand away.

And sometimes he'll call with almost *nothing* because he can't stand the idea that you might be stealing the pot, even though nobody has seen you bluff since last Thursday.

Sometimes he will have no alternative but to fold. Then he goes crazy, because what if it was *this* time that you were stealing?[3]

---

[2]Dominated hand theory again.

[3]You will almost assuredly get called the next time.

If you get check-raised in this situation, you can almost always throw away a single pair, calling just enough to remind your opponents that you're not guaranteed to do so. But that's not what happens most of the time — most of the time they say, "Nice hand" and you win the pot.

So, in the words of one of my mentors: "Close your eyes and fling your chips out there."

Quiz on Post-Flop Play

1. Give three reasons why the flop is the most crucial point in a hold'em hand.

2. What is the most common mistake made by low-limit hold'em players on the flop?

3. What is the most important use of the check-raise in low-limit hold'em games?

4. How should you normally play A♠-Q♠ if the flop comes Q♦-J♥-2♣ and you were the only one who raised before the flop?

5. How should you normally play A♠-5♠ in late position if the flop comes A♥-8♦-4♣, there has been no raise before the flop, and you have six opponents?

6. How should you normally play Q♥-Q♣ in early position against five opponents if the flop comes A♣-T♦-4♦ and there was one raise pre-flop?

7. If you have T♦-9♦ and the flop comes T♣-9♠-4♣, what should you do, and why?

8. Suppose you have K♥-K♦, you have raised before the flop, and six players take the flop, which comes K♣-7♦-2♥. What should you normally do?

9. You have A♣-T♣ on the button. Six people take the flop, which comes J♣-9♦-4♣. There's a bet and three calls in front of you. What should you normally do?

10. You have 9♥-8♥ in late position. There is no raise pre-flop, and five people take the flop, which comes T♦-6♣-3♣. It is checked until the player to your right bets. What should you normally do? Now assume the same situation, but there was one raise pre-flop. What should you normally do?

11. Suppose you have T♣-T♦ in middle position, there is a raise before the flop and five callers. The flop comes T♥-8♥-8♠. How should you normally play? What would be a reasonable alternative play?

12. Suppose you have 5♠-3♦ on the big blind and get to see the flop for "free." The flop comes 4♣-7♣-6♥. You have four opponents. How should you normally play?

13. You have J♦-T♦ on the button and are the fourth caller (no raise). The flop comes 7♣-6♥-2♥. There is a bet and one call in front of you. How should you normally play? Now suppose the flop comes 9♣-4♥-2♦. How does this change the situation?

14. You have 6♠-5♠ in middle position with four opponents, and no raise pre-flop. The flop comes T♣-6♥-3♣. There's a bet and a caller in front of you. What is typically the best play in this situation?

15. You have A♦-A♠ in late position and raise before the flop, ending up with two opponents. The flop comes K♣-T♣-4♦. The first player to act bets, the second folds. You raise and the first player makes it three bets. What would be reasonable plays in this situation?

16. You have Q♣-J♠ on the big blind, and there are five callers including you. The flop comes 8♥-J♦-2♥. You check, as does everybody else until the last player to act, who bets. You check-raise, and the original bettor is the only one to call. Now the T♣ comes on the turn. What should you normally do?

17. You have A♥-9♥ on the button and are one of six callers. The flop comes A♣-3♦-8♣. You bet and get two callers. The turn is the 6♠ — they check, you bet, and they call. The river card is the J♣ and again they both check. What's probably your best play here?

18. You have A♥-K♦, you raise under the gun, and get three callers. The flop comes 7♥-K♣-3♠. You check, planning to check-raise, but it's checked around. The turn is the J♥, you bet and get one caller. The river is the 8♠. Should you bet or check, and why?

Answers to Quiz on Post-Flop Play

1. a) The flop determines the likely winner of the hand.

    b) It is when you must make a crucial play/no-play decision.

    c) (In structured-limit play only) you can gain information using cheaper bets that will allow you to make the correct decisions on later, more expensive, cards.

2. Calling bets and raises with hands that have little or no chance of winning the pot.

3. To force players to call two bets instead of one, often making it incorrect for them to call at all.

4. Aggressively. Raise or check-raise. Assume you have the best hand until somebody represents something better.

5. You have to play very cautiously. Against this many players, there's an excellent chance that somebody else has an ace with a better kicker. If there is a raise, you should get out. If there is a bet and a couple of calls, you should *probably* get out. If it's checked to you, go ahead and bet, hoping to win the pot right there.

6. Unfortunately, you can be almost sure that you're beaten. In spite of the large pot size, you should normally check, and fold if there's a bet. As you get to later position, if it's checked to you, it might be worth an exploratory bet. If you get called there, then you probably shouldn't invest any more money in the pot.

7. You should play very fast. Do whatever is necessary to get lots of bets in on the flop. While you almost assuredly have the best hand, there could be some very big draws out against you, and you want them to pay heavily to draw.

8. You should bet or raise immediately on the flop. The flop is just about perfect for you — it's virtually impossible

you won't have the best hand on the turn. However, there is so much money in the pot, there's no reason to slow-play. Furthermore, after you raised pre-flop, your opponents will expect you to bet, so you haven't given out any information.

9.   Normally you should raise. You are about a 2:1 dog to make your flush, so you are actually raising for value here. Also, your raise may get you a free card on the turn, should you need one. Note also that an eight or queen on the turn gives you an open-end straight draw as well; you may be able to bet your draw for value on the turn.

10.   In the first case, you can't call with your gutshot straight draw — there are not enough bets in the pot, and you must worry about a raise behind you or a check-raise in front. If there was a raise before the flop, you can usually call because the pot has gotten so large.

11.   You have flopped a monster hand, and the chance of your being beaten is tiny. However, the pot is huge (10 small bets on the flop), so there's probably no point in slow-playing. On the other hand, slow-playing this hand is a reasonable approach — you're not worried about getting beaten, and you're willing to let some lesser hands catch up.

12.   In spite of a relatively small pot, you must do everything you can to eliminate opponents immediately. You could be up against a club flush draw or a big straight draw (such as 9♥-8♥). It's even possible you're dead against 85, but that's unlikely. You must bet and/or raise on the flop.

13.   Even though you have two overcards, you should normally fold. You have no backdoor flush chances, and the 7-6 combination on the flop makes two pair more likely. In the second situation, you have backdoor straight and flush chances and there's perhaps less chance that you're already up against two pair. You can call a bet here.

14. You've missed the flop — your second pair with no kicker is useless. Fold immediately.

15. You could call and then call your opponent's bets on the turn and river (assuming he bets). It's possible he has already made two pair or a set, but with this flop you can't fold yet. On the other hand, if you suspect your opponent is raising with a king or a draw, you could raise once more and try to regain control of the hand, forcing him to check on the turn. An alternative is to call and then raise on the turn.

16. You should probably bet out. You may run into two pair or even a straight, but you have to take that chance on the turn. You don't dare give a heart flush draw a free card, or a jack with a smaller kicker a free card with which to beat you. On the river, you should usually check, since now there are no "free" cards to give, and you're not sure if you want to be called or not.

17. You should typically check. As in the above situation, the board is fairly scary, and you just have one pair with a mediocre kicker. If you bet and get called, you can't be very happy. If an opponent bets into you on the end, you should call. If the river card were the J♦ instead of the flush-completing club, you should bet.

18. Go ahead and bet here. There are many worse hands that will call you. The flop that got checked around may confuse some people; you will probably get called by a worse king and maybe even a jack.

Section III

Miscellaneous
Topics
Bibliography
Glossary
Index

♠ ♥ ♦ ♣

Player Stereotypes

Y ou will quickly learn that you spend a relatively small percentage of your time at the poker table actually playing a hand. The dealer spends time shuffling the cards and dealing, selling chips, etc. Furthermore, after reading much of this book, you've discovered that you don't get to play very many of the hands you're dealt. So, what do you do when you're not in a hand?

Study your opponents and the way they play.

While each player has his own playing style, there are some general categories into which most players fall. Understanding these categories will help you know how to play against different kinds of players.

Loose-passive — the "calling station"

This is one of the best kind of players to have in your game. He has learned that any two cards can win in hold'em, and he would hate to be out of the pot if his hand would have been a winner. He will call before the flop with just about any two cards. Often, he will continue calling throughout the rest of the hand until it is inescapably obvious that he can't win. Furthermore, the loose-passive player won't do much raising. Mostly, he calls. An important point: it is virtually useless to try to bluff him — he'll call no matter what hand you represent.

Now here's the *really* good news: a large percentage of the players you play against in low-limit hold'em games will be loose-passive. They will occasionally catch some miracle draws to make very good hands, but over the long haul, they will steadily give away their chips.

Loose-aggressive — the "maniac"

The loose-aggressive player is much more difficult to handle. He too plays a lot of hands, but he likes to raise a lot. He'll raise with any ace, or any two suited cards. If there is a re-raise behind him, he'll often say, "Cap it!"[1] with little regard for his cards. He wants to *gamble*. On later betting rounds, he'll bet and raise with anything, hoping to scare people out of the pot. He *loves* to bluff.

This kind of player will eventually lose his money, too. He plays too many hands that have no value, and bluffs in places where he has no hope of being successful. However, he will create much more confusion than the calling station, and he will win some pots through sheer bluster. When a maniac gets on a run of good (or lucky) cards, he can fill up chip racks as fast as the chip runners can bring them. A maniac can be very good for you if you have a good hand, because he will do all the betting for you. However, you will occasionally find yourself throwing away the best hand against this kind of player.

Furthermore, a maniac will greatly increase your variance.[2] He will be capping the betting pre-flop with almost random hands. A maniac or two at a table can make the pots humongous, but you'll have to risk a lot of chips to win one of them.

Tight-passive — the "rock"

This sort of player is perhaps most common in Las Vegas and Reno. Often, he'll be a retiree who can't afford to be throwing a lot of money around the table. He's played a few thousand hours, and has a pretty good idea of which hands are good and which are not. The rock doesn't like speculative hands and generally avoids fancy plays — he likes to "get two big cards and bet'em."[3] While these players are fairly predictable, you aren't likely to make a lot of money from them.

---

[1]"Cap" means to put in the last raise. If there are only three raises permitted, by putting in the third one, he "caps" the betting.

[2]"Variance" is a statistical term describing the swings you have away from your expected results. The higher the variance, the larger the up and down swings in your bankroll.

[3]This straightforward approach to hold'em success has been attributed to poker legend Johnny Moss (although Johnny was anything but a "rock").

Tight-aggressive — the solid player

This is the kind of player *you* want to be. He doesn't play very many hands, but when he does, he tends to take control. He will use the check-raise to freeze up bettors or cause weaker players to make playing mistakes. He will raise for value and to get free cards. He is aware of the pot odds at all times, and makes the correct play based on them.

This kind of player is dangerous. Optimally, you'd like to be the only player of this type at your table. If you see too many of them when you sit down, you should look for another table.

Categorizing your opponents

So how do you tell what kind of opponents you're up against?

Before you get into a game, stand on the rail and watch the players. Pick two players and watch them for two full rotations of the button around the table — about 20 hands. One saw the flop 19 times, never raising, but calling all the pre-flop raises. It's a fair guess that he's a calling station. The fellow next to him played in only three pots during that time, and raised once. It's harder to tell when somebody is playing a small number of hands, but you want to be more careful of the second player — he's (probably) being more selective about the cards he plays.

In the game, watch what players show down. Suppose a player raises pre-flop and then shows down 95s; that doesn't mean very much. But if he raises three times in 10 minutes and shows down similar hands every time, you may start to suspect that he's got maniacal tendencies. You can also learn things by hands players *don't* show down. For instance, if a player calls a bet on the end, and then throws away his hand when shown top pair, you know he couldn't beat it. What hands could he have had? Try to figure out what kinds of cards he was playing.

Note also that players can change categories, either intentionally or unconsciously. If they're doing it intentionally, look out. A player who knowingly shifts gears in his playing is one to be respected. However, a player may go "on tilt" because he's lost too many hands, too much money, or simply gotten too many good hands beaten. Then he can turn into a maniac for a while and start calling and raising with terrible hands. Be alert for this behavior so you can take advantage of it.

Bluffing and Implicit Collusion

Bluffing is rarely correct in low-limit hold'em games.

P lease go back and read that first sentence again. Now say it out loud. You may find this a surprising and disturbing statement. What is poker without bluffing? You needn't worry — there will be plenty of bluffing in your low-limit hold'em game. However, *you* should not be the one doing it. In this chapter, we will explain why.

If you get into a pot with one or two opponents, bluffing is an integral part of the game. However, in low-limit games, you rarely have one or two opponents — you have five or six or more. The probability of a bluff working against any one of them is perhaps quite high (in fact, you will normally have some of them beaten). However, the probability of your bluff working against *all* of them, which it must to succeed, is exceedingly low. We call this concept "implicit collusion." Effectively, the whole table is colluding against the bluffer (you) — *somebody* will call and catch your bluff.

In general, for a bluff to be correct, you must believe it will be successful often enough to pay for itself. Suppose all the cards are out and you have missed your flush draw. Now it's checked to you, the last player to act. There are 15 big bets in the pot. Your bluff, if it works, will win 15 bets for you. If unsuccessful (i.e., you are called), you lose one bet. So your bluff must succeed once in every 16 tries to be a break-even proposition. If it succeeds more than that, you are making money; less than that, you are losing. Against a lot of players, even 15:1 on your bluff may not be sufficient. The implicit collusion effect, especially if the pot is large, will overwhelm the value of your bluff.

When should you bluff?

Very rarely.

That said: you should do it when the pot has been limited to a very few players, but is quite large. Suppose you have

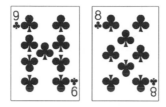

in late position. Four players call in front of you, as do you. The little blind raises, a player in the middle re-raises, you call the other two bets. Now the little blind caps the betting and everybody calls. There are 24 small bets in the pot before the dealer has put out the flop, which comes

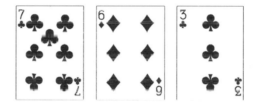

The little blind bets and gets three callers. You raise and everybody calls. That's 10 more small bets for a total of 34 bets. The turn is the 4♠. The little blind bets again, and you are the only caller. The river is the 2♦. Now the little blind checks. There are now 19 big bets in the pot — if the little blind will fold once in 20 hands like this, your bluff is worth it. However, if you suspect that the little blind actually has a *worse* hand than you (perhaps you have A♣-K♣ instead of 9♣-8♣), you should check the hand down. This is because you might run into a check-raise bluff and you can't call.

Remember, however, many players will not fold once in a *hundred* times like this. When up against such a player, save the last bet and check the hand down, even if you have no hope of winning in the showdown.

Catching a bluff

Some players seem to get a huge rush from bluffing, and will do it in spite of being caught on a regular basis. In bigger games, you might have to make a stand once in a while to catch them. However, in a low-limit game, your fellow players are acting as an ad hoc posse against this potential pot thief. You should feel no reason to participate. If you think the pot odds justify a call, do so, but don't call simply to "keep him honest."

Once in a while, you will get caught bluffing and *still win*. This is another strange phenomenon of low-limit poker. A player will decide to catch your bluff and call — but without cards strong enough to beat your bluff. When this happens, you have gained enormously. Not only have you gained the advertising value of the bluff, but you still win the pot. Because of this behavior, you should bluff with the strongest of your bad hands and missed draws.

Of course, you should *never* call if you can't beat a bluff. If you are certain your opponent is bluffing, but you can't beat a bluff, you must raise and hope that he will fold. This is a very high variance play and you must use it sparingly. It is a classic situation where the only reasonable choices are fold and raise — you cannot call.

Getting caught bluffing

On those rare occasions when you *do* try a bluff, you will occasionally get caught. Many players, for some reason, immediately throw their hands away in this situation. They are giving away the one advantage of being caught when they're bluffing — advertisement. Your opponents will remember your bluffs far better if you show them down, and then will be more inclined to call you when you have a big hand.

You might even consider announcing your hand: "There — beat that pair of fours!" It might make your opponents remember your rare bluff that much better.

A final thought on bluffing

In *Super/System*, his extraordinary poker text, Doyle Brunson says the following:

> **If you're in a *loose* game, where the first man is as likely to have 7-6 as A-K, and where almost every pot is being raised, you can normally *forget about* putting people on hands before the Flop. You can also *forget about* doing anything "fancy". You're going to have to show down the best hand to win. That's all there is to it.**

Doyle is still right.

More thoughts on implicit collusion

This concept is very powerful, especially in low-limit games where you are constantly trying to outrun a lot of opponents. Another example is raising with the second best hand to limit the field to you and a single opponent. Sometimes if a player bets, you should raise even if you're fairly sure he has you beaten. Suppose he has a 40% chance to win the pot, you have a 30% chance, and the last 30% is spread out over three other opponents. Now he bets and you raise, forcing the three opponents behind you to fold. You have both benefited from this play — perhaps he has a 60% chance to win now and you have 40%. If there were originally 12 bets in the pot when he bet, you clearly should call if you have a 30% chance of winning. However, if you put in an extra bet (raise) and increase your chance of winning to 40%, you have gained more than the cost of that extra bet.

Spread Limit Games

First let's discuss how a spread limit game works. In a typical Las Vegas spread limit $1-4-8-8 game, there is a big blind of $2 and a little blind of $1. It's $2 to call before the flop, but you can raise $4, making it $6 to go. On the flop, you can bet any dollar amount from $1 to $4, and $1-$8 on the last two rounds. Finally, a raise must be at least as large as any previous bet or raise on that round.

In practice, these games end up playing like structured games with a very small pre-flop bet because most players (correctly) bet the maximum on each betting round following the flop.

Buy low, sell high

This well known piece of stock market advice applies to spread limit poker games too. When you are drawing, you would like to be calling small bets ("buying low"), but once you have the best hand, you want to charge your opponents the highest possible price to catch up with you ("sell high").

Therefore, if you think you have the best hand, bet the maximum permitted; pretend it's a structured game and that's the *only* amount you're allowed to bet. If you're drawing at a straight or a flush, you hope your opponents choose to bet less than the maximum, which they will do sometimes. For instance, an opponent may bet a small amount with top pair but a bad kicker. This is a mistake. If you believe you should bet, then you should bet the maximum, otherwise check.

Some of your opponents will continue to bet a dollar or two when they could bet as much as eight. Sadly, this sort of incorrect play has become rare, but you may see it once in a while. When an opponent gives you such a bargain, you can draw at many more hands, and when you make them, you charge your opponent full price to see the result. For instance, if there is $12 in the pot with one card to come, and your opponent bets just $1, you can call with an inside straight draw! Of course, if you do

148

this, be sure you are drawing at the nuts, since some players will bet less than the maximum to draw you in when they have an unbeatable hand.

Since some people adjust their bet size to their perceived quality of their hand, you get wonderful information. If they bet a little, they have an "OK" hand. If they bet a lot, they have a "good" hand. If somebody is doing this, he is probably not a very experienced poker player; be careful what information you try to glean from his actions. What he thinks is a good hand and what you do might be very different.

Also, the bigger the range of permitted bets, the more drastic the difference between big pairs and drawing hands. For instance, $2-10 (on all four betting rounds) used to be a common spread limit structure and is still found occasionally today. If you see the flop for $2, and then flop top pair, you can make it wildly incorrect for opponents to draw to straights and flushes by betting $10 on the flop. Many players did not understand the dramatic shift in value caused by this wide betting range. The result was that the bad players lost their money very quickly and the games dried up. Limits such as $1-4-8-8 have less latitude, and have pot odds situations that more closely resemble structured games.

Seeing cheap flops

The biggest change in a $1-4-8-8 game from a $4-8 or $3-6 game is that you can see many more flops because of the lower price and high implied odds. You still have to watch your position, because a $4 raise destroys the implied odds you were hoping to get by sneaking in for $2. But as you get to middle position, you can start to play almost any hand that can flop big, assuming you can do it for one bet. Any suited ace, king, queen, or jack. Any suited connector, one-gap, or two-gap. Any pair.

Pot odds

Some drawing hands that are easy calls post-flop in "structured" games (e.g., $3-$6) are not as clear in spread limit. Since the post-flop bet may be as much as two or four times the pre-flop bet, you must think about your odds before calling with a draw.

Sometimes you can use the bet size to minimize an investment you're not altogether happy about making. Perhaps you're on the button and have flopped the nut flush draw in a $1-4-8-8 spread limit game. Now there's a bet of $2 in front of you and one caller. You'd like to get a free card on the turn if necessary, but there aren't enough people in the pot to make a raise for value correct. Therefore, you might raise $2. This is a common enough practice (raising the bet size rather than the maximum) that it shouldn't attract too much attention. However, it may make the original bettor check on the turn.

The exception?

You might think that you could bet less when you have an unbeatable hand, hoping to get more callers. This might occasionally be correct on the river when you're trying to "sell" a very big hand. However, in general, you shouldn't do this — you're just giving away information about how good your hand is, just as the novice players do when they bet good hands big and OK hands small.

Bet the maximum with your beatable *and* unbeatable hands — let your opponents guess which one you have.

Poker and Computers

Disclaimer: It's hopeless to write about "current" computer usage in a book with an intended useful life of more than about a year. Therefore, please treat this chapter as a sample of what things are like at the time of writing — the summer of 2000.

Since 1994, when Roy Hashimoto and I wrote the first edition of this book, personal computer usage around the world has exploded. Terms such as Internet and email have become a standard part of our language overnight. Of course, that means that computers are being used to learn about poker, discuss poker, and even play poker.

Computer simulation

Bob Wilson's *Turbo Texas Hold'em* is the first program that allows poker players to simulate anything like actual play. You can program a large number of player profiles using dozens of parameters for each profile, and then play against those players or have them play against themselves. While playing against "TTH" opponents is not the same as the real thing, it's a wonderful way for a hold'em novice to get his feet wet. Also, many poker theorists have spent hundreds of hours trying to learn more about the game using TTH (Las Vegas pro Abdul Jalib has widely published his results). Either way, every serious student of the game should have this software. You can find out more about it at www.wilsonsw.com.

Discussing poker online

There are two places on the Internet that have serious poker discussions. The oldest is the rec.gambling.poker Usenet newsgroup. Like most of Usenet, the original topic (poker theory and practice) has been heavily diluted by random chat, flames, and other ills. However, you can still learn a thing or two there, and they're quite tolerant of newcomers asking basic questions.

More recently, the poker forums on the Two Plus Two Publishing website (www.twoplustwo.com) have taken over the serious discussion of how to play various hands. Well known poker player/ writers Mason Malmuth and David Sklansky run the website and contribute frequently to the discussions. You may find those discussions a bit heavy going when you first start playing the game, but they are fascinating reading once you start worrying about the more subtle points of hold'em.

Playing poker over the Internet

For many years, computer-literate poker players have played against each other using the Internet Relay Chat (IRC) service. The most popular venue for IRC poker is irc.poker.net, hosted at the website www.poker.net.[1]

However, a handful of commercial companies have set up their own poker servers to allow people to play against each other over the Internet, both for play and *real* money. At this writing, the two most popular commercial poker sites are Paradise Poker (www.paradisepoker.com) and Planet Poker (www.planet-poker.com).

Is it a good idea to play poker on the Internet?

The jury is still out.[2] As I write this, online poker for real money is less than a year old. It has boomed in popularity, particularly among those who can't easily get to cardrooms. Even among those who can, many people prefer the comfort, convenience, and anonymity of playing poker in their spare bedroom any time they want.

---

[1]Chris Ferguson, who won the final event at the 2000 World Series of Poker, learned many of his tactics playing tournaments on IRC. He readily acknowledges the value that all that computer practice time had for him.

[2]This is where my disclaimer at the top really matters. I am virtually certain that a year from now, online poker will look nothing like it does today. I'm not sure how, but there will be big changes.

The obvious concern here is collusion. It is trivial for two or three people to "sit" at the same online poker table and freely converse (over the phone, Internet, or sitting in the same physical room) about what they're doing. Furthermore, they don't even need to be particularly aggressive about their collusion. Simply playing only the best hand among the two or three they collectively have provides some edge. I will go only a little way out on a limb here and say that I'm virtually certain that some amount of such collusion is taking place in online poker.

That said, I believe that the commercial poker sites want clean games (they're making plenty of money in the rake). Whether they have the technology and will to detect and eliminate collusion is yet to be seen.

Of course, there's some collusion going on in real (as opposed to virtual) cardrooms. Is it less than the Internet poker sites? I'm inclined to believe it is simply because doing it online is so easy and foolproof. I don't have any more than anecdotal evidence of that, but that's my sense of the matter.

Finally, to further confuse matters, some people are beating Internet poker for substantial amounts of money. I *don't* believe that the collusion problem is so bad that a very good player can't make a healthy profit.

The jury is still out.

Tournaments

Unlike regular "ring" or "live" games, poker tournaments are played with chips that have no cash value. You pay a certain amount of money, known as the "buy-in," and receive tournament chips in exchange. The number of tournament chips you receive doesn't necessarily have any correlation to the amount of money you paid - just think of them as points.

A tournament starts with blinds of a certain level, and then increases those blinds at regular intervals, often doubling them for the first few rounds. As the blind levels increase, players with smaller stacks are quickly forced all-in, and one by one, people bust out. In some tournaments, a player may buy in again ("rebuy") during the first few blind levels[1]. Otherwise, he is out of the tournament.

In most tournaments, there is a percentage payout. That is, the tournament continues until one person has won all the chips, but the last few people each get a percentage of the total prize pool.

For instance, 100 people might each put up $60 to participate in a limit hold'em tournament. Of that $60, $10 goes to the cardroom or casino that is hosting the tournament, and $50 goes into the prize pool, so there's $5000 in the prize pool. Each player receives 500 in tournament chips, and the blinds start at 5 and 10, so the game plays like a regular 10-20 hold'em game. After 30 minutes, the blinds double - now they're 10 and 20, and the game is a 20-40 structure. This continues with the more fortunate players building big stacks and the less fortunate ones busting out. Let's say that our sample tournament has rebuys during the first three blind levels, and 48 players took 57 $50 rebuys (note that some players rebought multiple times). The additional $2850 (57 x $50) is added to the prize pool for a total of $7850.

---

[1] I hold with the school that says that the tournament starts when the rebuys end.

154

Before the tournament begins, the hosting club announces the prize structure. For our example, a typical structure might be 40% to the winner, 20% to 2nd place, 10% to third place, 5% to places 4-7, and 3.3% to places 8-10. So the person who busts out when there are six people left in the tournament wins 5% of the total prize pool, or about $390 — not a bad return on a $50 investment (plus any rebuys that player made).[2]

It's these big wins that make tournaments wildly popular. Of course, many of those people will sit down in regular games when they bust out of the tournament, and that makes the cardroom happy.

Tournaments have become such a big thing that some people play tournaments exclusively and don't play in ring games. There are even tournament professionals who follow the tournament trail around the country, hoping to make a single big win that will keep them in buy-in's (and groceries) for the next 6-12 months.

Cheap tournaments as practice

Many players like the cheap buy-in tournaments ($25 or less) because it allows them to play a lot of poker and get a lot of experience for a limited amount of money. And, of course, they might just hit a run of cards and make a profit.

I think this is an excellent approach if you have a limited bankroll and have gotten everything you can out of Turbo Texas Hold'em and free online poker.

No tournament strategy tips here

I'm not a tournament expert and don't pretend to be one, so I'm not going to give any advice about how to play in one. Realize though, that particularly toward the end of the tournament, proper strategy may vary dramatically from that for a ring game. For instance, in a percentage payout tournament, it may be correct to

---

[2]Not as good a return as the ultimate winner makes; he collects $3140, less taxes.

avoid playing a hand even though you have the best hand, if staying out of the hand gives you the chance to move up in the payout ladder. Many good tournament players will argue that there are times when you should fold pocket aces pre-flop. More specifically, you should fold without looking at your cards because you have the highest expectation by staying out of the hand and hoping one or more opponents bust out on that hand.

The degree to which correct tournament play differs from correct ring game play is a hotly debated topic in the poker community, but everybody agrees that the two are different. If you decide to be a serious tournament player, you'll have to study books about tournament poker and, of course, watch the best players and learn from them.

♠   ♥   ♦   ♣

Rakes and Tokes

U nfortunately, when you play poker in a public cardroom or casino, there are two taxes that you pay throughout your session: the rake and tokes.

Rakes

As we discussed before, the house makes its money in one of three ways:

1. It "rakes" an amount of money from each pot, typically 5%-10% of the pot with a maximum rake per pot.

2. It charges a fixed amount to the player who has the button each hand. That money is removed from the table, but sometimes counts as a blind bet for the player.

3. It collects a "time" charge, normally every half hour, from each player at the table.

Many players prefer the rake method — they argue that the winners are paying the house because the money comes out of the pot. If you don't win pots, you don't pay any rake.

We will discuss this idea below.

Tokes

In most public cardrooms, you are generally expected to tip the dealer when you win a pot. This is called a "toke" — short for "token." The typical amount varies — in Nevada cardrooms, $.50 to $1 is average. In wild and wooly California $3-$6 games, we have seen players routinely toke as much as $5 for large pots, but $1 is the normal amount.[1]

Is toking necessary? Unfortunately, dealers are paid very little (sometimes minimum wage) and earn most of their money from

---

[1]Note that if you play online (see "Playing poker over the Internet" beginning on page 152) you don't toke. For a low-limit player, this is a significant financial factor.

157

tokes. Thus, for the foreseeable future, toking will be a part of the game. Given that you know this, it seems rather discourteous not to toke. However, you do not have to toke $5 in a $3-$6 hold'em game. Try to toke an amount that is customary for the game in which you're playing. I personally toke better dealers more, regardless of the quality of cards they give me; I'm making my own small attempt to "pay for performance."

Tax reduction hint

As you can see, a toke is a tax on your pot. If the pot is raked (rather than time being collected on the button or every half hour), that is a further tax. If player A wins $500 in four pots, and player B wins $500 in ten pots, A pays only 40% of the tax that B does, and has a greater net win. This is yet another reason to play tight but aggressive poker — you don't want to win a lot of pots, you want to win a lot of money.

Now let's go back to the statement that raking a pot is good for the players since the winners pay the rake. You may routinely win fewer *pots* than the average player, and yet win more *money* than he does. You'll be selective about the pots you enter, and you will win a much greater percentage of those pots. Therefore, having the pot raked *is* good for you, but may not be good for the average player who makes that statement.

Play extra tight if the pot is raked

If money is removed from the pot via a rake or button charge, you must play more tightly than if you pay time on the half-hour. That's because some of the money that you collect by winning the pot is *gone*. If your game is a $2-4 or $3-6, and they're taking 5% up to $3, then (on most pots) the entire 5% is gone before you can get your hands on it. A fixed button charge of $3 is an even bigger bite out of your potential profit (if the pot stays under $60). So if there is money being taken from the pot, be more conservative about your starting hand requirements. Avoid the marginal hands (which isn't a bad idea anyway) and just play quality cards.

♠   ♥   ♦   ♣

Bankroll Considerations

Many players play with too few chips in front of them.

You will occasionally hear players say that they like playing with "short stacks" (not many chips for the size of the game) because that way they can get all-in and not have to make decisions. However, poker is all about decisions. If you don't want to make decisions, don't play poker.

If you are a good poker player, you want to have plenty of chips in front of you for two reasons:[1]

1. If you make a big hand and are fortunate enough to be up against somebody who made a big (but not quite as good) hand, you want to get full value for your hand. If your opponent check-raises you on the turn with the worst hand, putting you all-in, you've missed at least two or three big bets that you should have won on that hand.

2. Not having to make a decision since you're all-in is *not* a benefit. If you are a better poker player than your opponents, your decisions are better and you can raise or fold as appropriate. If you are all-in, you are effectively reduced to calling, and can't force opponents out with check-raises, etc.

How much do you need at the table?

In a $3-$6 or $1-$4-$8-$8 game, you should start with at least $80 or $100, and have another $100 or $200 ready to put into play. In a $3-$6 structured game with a three raise maximum, it will cost you $72 (12 big bets) to cover three raises on all four betting rounds. Of course, this is an exceptional case, but sometimes you make a huge hand and have one or more people calling

---

[1]For the curious reader, there are circumstances in which you have an advantage with a short stack. Malmuth and Sklansky have both written about this situation, but it is beyond the scope of this text. Furthermore, most players handle short stacks very poorly.

or raising. In that case, you want to extract maximum value. If the game is wild and there is a lot of raising, you should have the entire 12 big bets, or close to it. If the game is very tight and there's not a lot of raising, you can play with as few as seven or eight big bets.

Since the game is table stakes, you won't be permitted to go into your pocket for more money during the hand, so you must have the maximum you'd want to bet in front of you before the hand starts.

You will often see your opponents buying into the game for the minimum — perhaps $20 or $30. Each time they bust out (and they seem to do that frequently), they re-buy for that same amount. Furthermore, players who buy in this manner often want to gamble with just those few chips. They will raise or re-raise in an attempt to get all-in early in the hand, almost regardless of their cards. Be aware of this sort of behavior — in that case you can't play marginal hands or draws because you'll have to pay lots of money for them early. Play premium big cards and pairs. Note also that when a player is all-in, implied odds cease to exist. If you make a drawing hand, he has no money with which to pay you off. Therefore, when drawing against a player who is all-in, you must be getting correct pot odds right there.

Finally, you can almost *never* bluff a player off his last couple of chips. Don't bother trying.

How much do you need in your bankroll?

The answer to this question is not as simple as the one above. For instance, you may think of your bankroll as a completely separate financial entity that may be added to or removed from only at the poker table. If this is your view, then Mason Malmuth's research suggests you need about 300 big bets ($1800 for a $3-6 player) to ride out the inevitable downward swings.[2]

---

[2]If, of course, you're a winning player. If you're a losing player, no bankroll is big enough.

However, many people don't separate it out. If they have a few extra dollars, they might go play some poker. If they win, fine. If they lose, that's okay too. If that's how you prefer to manage your money, then you don't need a particular bankroll size - you simply replenish it (or withdraw from it) as you see fit.

By the way, I find the former approach (a separate bucket labeled "poker bankroll") to be an excellent disciplinary tool. Even if your financial circumstances permit you to add to the bankroll, it's healthy to monitor its growth (and shrinking), and keeping it separate will make that possible. It also attenuates the emotional swings associated with wins and losses. If you don't view a win as, "Oh boy, a new stereo!" or a loss as, "Oh dear, what of the rent?" then you'll play a better poker game all around.

I should note that I have many friends who have parlayed very small bankrolls in the $2-4 and $3-6 games into five-figure bankrolls with which they're playing serious mid-limit poker. This is not easy, and demands time, work, and a little luck. But if you start out with a reasonable bankroll for your low limit game (so you don't go busted when you lose a few times) then you, too, can do it.

Tips for Playing in a Public Cardroom

If you've been playing poker in a home game and decide to play in a public cardroom or casino, there are some rules and conventions of which you're probably not aware. Some of these are generally observed, some of them are written rules. You will find your fellow players in a cardroom to be generally friendly people, but they will be unforgiving about rules violations — and ignorance of those rules is no excuse. Learn these now and it will save you a lot of grief (and a pot or two) in the future.

- When you first sit down at the game, you may be allowed to be dealt in immediately, or you may be forced to post an amount equal to the big blind. If so, wait until the button has just passed you and then post. If you post immediately *before* the blinds get to you, you will have to play the blinds very soon — you'd rather wait until they pass. This also gives you time to relax and watch the game for a few hands before you play.

- Protect your cards at all times. Keep your hand on them or put a chip or other weight on them. Otherwise, they may be fouled if folded cards hit them or the dealer accidentally picks them up. On a related subject, don't lift them up off the table. To look at them, cover them with your hands, and raise the corners slightly so you can see them. This will take a little practice, but will eventually become second nature.

- Act in turn. It's against the rules to act before it's your turn, even if you're just going to fold. Sometimes a player in front of you will act out of turn, causing you to act out of turn. Try to keep an eye on the action so you know when it really is your turn. On a related note, if the betting has been checked to you, check as well, even if you have every intention of folding at the first opportunity. Folding prematurely gives an unfair advantage to players behind you (they know *you* won't check-raise them), and is simply bad manners.

- When it's your turn to act, act as quickly on your hand as possible. If you need a few seconds to think about it, say "Time, please." This will stop the action at you so you can decide what to do. If you don't say "Time" and people act behind you, your hand may be declared dead.

- Unlike a home game, you do *not* put your chips directly into the pot. Put them in a neat stack in front of you (whether they be antes or bets). The dealer will collect them all together when he is persuaded the pot is right. If you just toss your chips into the pot, there may be a concern that you put too few in. If so, somebody may demand that the dealer count down the pot, and people will be upset with you.

- When you raise, say so before doing anything else. Otherwise, you must get all the chips for your raise into the pot with one motion. If you do not declare your raise and make a second trip to your stack for chips, you are making a "string bet" and may be required to just call. If you declare your raise verbally, you can take all the time you want to get the raise in.

- Don't fold at the end just because somebody declares a better hand than yours. Simply turn your hand over, and verify what you have. It is also the dealer's job to determine the winner, but you should check for yourself. Don't release your hand until you've seen one better than yours.

- Get in the habit of looking at your cards once and memorizing them. This will enable you to play more smoothly and concentrate on what you're doing. Any time you look back at your cards, it should be for show.

- In a table stakes game, you don't have to fold because you can't call an entire bet. Call with the rest of your chips, and the dealer will make a side pot.[1]

---

[1]See the glossary for more information about the terms "table stakes" and "side pot".

Discipline

Without discipline, you have no chance of being a winning poker player.

N o matter how hard you study the material in this book, the lessons you learn will be useless if you don't apply them. While that may seem easy in the comfort of your living room, it will be a very different situation when you are at the table in a public cardroom or casino.

There will be bright lights, noise, laughter, TV, smoke, music, and every other imaginable distraction around you. If you are playing in a Las Vegas style casino, there will be the incessant ringing, clanging, and beeping of slot machines. Also in Las Vegas, attractive young ladies will be offering you free liquor on a regular basis. The players at your table will be "gambling it up" — making the craziest draws, raising for fun, and capping the betting pre-flop by implicit or explicit agreement. If you follow the guidelines in this book, you will be folding hand after hand, almost like a robot. Every once in a while, you will get to the flop, and then much of the time you'll fold there. Occasionally when you get all the way to the river, somebody will hang in with a wildly improbable draw and beat the best hand you've made all evening.

And now you must go back to the question we asked at the beginning of the book: "What is your goal?"

If you want to get in and gamble with these folks, play a lot of pots, and make some of those miracle catches, feel free to do so. But if your goal is to *win the most money,* then you have only one choice. You play the hands that you know are good and throw away the trash. You fold AX in early position without hesitation before the flop. You stay with draws that offer you the correct odds, and dump the rest. You bet for value and rarely bluff. With time and practice, you will become a strong and dangerous poker player. You may not get much "respect" at the table — it's in very short supply at low-limit hold'em tables — but you won't care much. If they want to see your strong hand and are willing to pay for the privilege, fine.

Winning by folding

At the beginning of the book, we said that perhaps the most important lesson we could teach you was "when to fold." Throughout this text, we've tried to emphasize the importance of playing just good solid cards. If you follow our guidelines, you will be playing half or a third as many hands as your average opponent — maybe *fewer*. This means you won't be leaking chips away here and there in bad pots, and you will pay less pot tax.

Your opponents will probably not notice you very much because you won't be a major participant in the game. Mostly, you'll fold and watch. When you finally do come into a hand, you'll wonder how they can play with you because it must be obvious that you're starting out with better cards than they are. Don't worry — you'll get plenty of action.

When you stand up and cash out a healthy profit, they'll wonder how it happened — you didn't seem to be in many pots. No, you weren't in many pots, but you won a large percentage of the pots in which you *did* participate. This is what we mean when we say "winning by folding."

Going on tilt

This is one of the worst things that can happen to a poker player, yet it happens to all of us. You miss what seems like the twentieth straight flush draw, followed by the only big pair you've seen all night getting beaten by a runner-runner two pair. All of a sudden, your carefully developed game plan is gone, and you're playing every hand that comes along and staying in with flaky draws.

You're on tilt.

This is a good way to lose $300 instead of the $50 you were losing already. When you sense yourself heading in this direction, get up and leave. Very few of us have the energy and brilliance to play good poker while fighting for control of our game with our emotions. Go read a book, take a walk, have a bite to eat, but don't go back into your game until you are completely relaxed and under control.

Realize that you will have more bad beats put on you than you put on other players. The very definition of a bad beat means that a player should *not* have been in the hand, and yet caught a fluke card to beat the front-runner. You will not be in this situation very often. Either you will have the best hand going in, or you will be making a correct draw. Therefore, it may seem that you take more than an equitable share of bad beats. That's true, and it's a *good* thing.

Being nice to bad players

Along those lines, here is an important piece of advice: don't berate bad players. When a bad player makes an incredible catch to beat you, you will be tempted to explain to him (if not yell at him) exactly how lucky he was, that he only had two cards in the whole deck that would win the pot for him, and how could he call your raise cold on the turn?

Remember, it is the bad player from whom you make your money. If you get him upset, he may get out of a gambling mood or, worse, leave the table. Now you can't win his money. Astonishingly enough, this ill-mannered behavior toward lucky bad players is common. Instead, you should be particularly *nice* to bad players. When somebody puts a terribly bad beat on you, swallow, try to relax, and say in the calmest voice you can manage, "Good hand."

Also, berating bad players (or anybody, for that matter) is just poor manners.

Walking away a loser

You will *not* win every session.

However, many players find it extremely difficult to walk away from the table a loser, especially if they were winning earlier in the session. David Sklansky probably said it best: "It's all one big session." What he meant, of course, is that there's nothing magic about a specific session between the times that you walked in and out of a card club. Your goal, we hope, is to win as much money as possible *over the long term*. If the game is good and you feel good, continue playing. If the game has turned bad, you're not playing your best, or you have a dinner date with a friend, get up and walk away without a second thought.

Of course, never put a single dollar on the table that you can't afford to lose (i.e. don't play with the rent money). You must treat the chips as tokens, and not the groceries for tomorrow. You will not be able to play your best game with money you *need* — not to mention the fact that it's just poor financial management.

Playing loose and crazy in hopes of cashing out a winner is a good first step to going on tilt.

When should I stop playing?

One of the first questions new players ask is: "When should I get up from a session?" There are two different answers, depending on whether you look at the question statistically or psychologically.

Statistically speaking, if you are playing with an edge — that is, you are a winning player — there is no optimal time to stand up and leave; every minute you sit there you are making money. This means that if you are in a good game and are playing well, you should continue playing, whether you're ahead $500 or losing $500. Note also that if you are a losing player, then there is no optimal time to *sit down* — there is no way for you to beat the game.

The psychological answer is much more complex, and varies for each person. Some of us play our best when we're winning, and poorly when we're losing. For others, it's the exact opposite. You may find that when you're winning you play your best game

—this is a powerful combination. On the other hand, you may start to play looser and less carefully, eventually giving back your winnings. Dealing with losing is even more difficult. Some people tighten up and play their best when they're behind. Conversely, Mike Caro discusses the concept of "threshold of misery," a point past which you don't care how much you lose. If you're susceptible to such an effect, you must have a stop-loss limit, even though such a thing makes no statistical sense.

Folding

Early in the book, we told you that we'd teach you to win by folding. As we approach the end of this text, it's probably well to review some of the reasons that you should fold. So, you should be looking for a reason to fold if:

1. You look at your first two cards and *don't* think, "Hey, cool."

2. There's a raise in front of you pre-flop.

3. On the flop, you don't have top pair or better, an open-end straight draw, or four-card flush draw.

4. An unimaginative player raises on the turn and you don't have the pot odds to outdraw him if you're behind.

5. On the river, you have a marginal calling hand but there are other callers in front of you, or players to act behind you.

Of course, you shouldn't fold in *every* one of these situations, nor should you necessarily call if none of these apply. But these guidelines will help you get out of hands that are likely to cost you money.

Here's a tip about folding pre-flop: many experienced poker players will encourage you to not look at your cards until the action gets to you. This does indeed insure that you won't give away any tells to the other players before you act. However, I think that when you're new to the game, you're better off looking at your cards *immediately*. If for no other reason, it will give you time to find the reasons to fold. Often our first instinct is to put money in the pot; a little time to think may allow you to find an important reason to wait for the next hand.

Conclusion

W e wish we could say that now that you've read this book, you are a good or great low-limit hold'em player. Unfortunately, that's probably not true. However, we can say:

You now have the tools you need to become an excellent low-limit hold'em player.

Study, study, study

From here, you start your real education, playing as much hold'em as you can. Read this book again, and the books that we recommend in the next chapter. When a hand or a session goes badly, stop and think about what happened. Did you play poorly or did the other players get lucky? Remember, it's very easy to put the blame for bad results on others, but you should review your own play carefully first.

Begin to develop the talents you need to perfect your play at low-limit and to move up to bigger and tougher games. As we said in the introduction, there is no recipe for winning at hold'em. Learn to make the right decision most of the time. When should you raise with that gut shot straight draw and when should you throw it away? Review your mistakes and learn from them. When you got your flush beaten by a bigger one, could you have lost one fewer bet? Watch your opponents constantly. Why are they at the table? Are they happy and gambling, or are they intense, focused players like you? Are they playing on short stacks or do they have a lot of chips? Does the player in seat five know what a free card play is? The player in seat seven is having a snifter of brandy. Is that his first or fourth? How does his play change when he gets some alcohol in him? It's a lot to notice and take in, but you won't be playing many hands — you'll have *plenty* of time to watch and study your opponents.

Talk to your fellow poker buddies. Discuss hands with them and how you might have played them differently. Learn who the good players are and watch them — you will undoubtedly pick up a few tricks (though it may cost you a few bets).

Then advance

If you want to move up to higher stakes, we encourage you to do so, once you can beat the low-limit games regularly over an extended period of time (hundreds of hours). Then be sure to read Sklansky and Malmuth's *Hold'em Poker for Advanced Players* before advancing to the bigger games.

You may be tempted to advance to a bigger game after two or three straight sessions in which you win a lot of money. Note that the swings in poker, *particularly* the wilder low-limit games, are huge and inevitable. Three straight winning sessions are not a guarantee that you're ready to move up, nor are three straight losing sessions a guarantee that you should give up the game.

Above all, maintain a positive attitude and discipline. Those are the key components of becoming a winning low-limit hold'em player.

Afterword

I can't end this book without some comment about poker and perspective.

When Chris Ferguson (2000 World Series of Poker World Champion) and I were discussing possible quotes for him to contribute to the back of the second edition, we agreed that our favorite was:

> *Surely you have something better to do with your time than play poker. I suggest a walk outside, volunteering at a homeless shelter, or listening to Bach.*

It didn't make the back cover, but it deserved inclusion in this text.

Poker is a wonderful game and a delightful diversion. But it is not a substitute for life, and I see far too many people for whom it *is* life. Don't let yourself be one of those people.

Care for your family, friends, and neighbors. Get outside as much as possible. Tend to your spiritual needs, whatever they may be. Listen to good music. I commend to you Palestrina, the aforementioned Bach, Jerry Douglas, and Ladysmith Black Mambazo, but listen to whatever moves your soul. Read good books. I like mysteries, particularly Sharyn McCrumb and Ellis Peters. Chris Ferguson is a James Clavell fan. Be an informed citizen and use your vote.

Stay well, and thank you for reading our book.

Bibliography

Following are a few of our favorite poker books. Some of them will provide information that you absolutely *must* have to beat higher limit poker games. Some of them are just great stories. All are worth reading.

Alvarez, A. *The Biggest Game In Town.* Houghton Mifflin, 1983. (Paperback 1985). This book is a true story about Las Vegas and high-limit poker players. You will not learn a thing about how to play better poker, but this is a must read for poker players.[1]

Brunson, D. *Super/System.* B & G Publishing, 1978. This is the "Bible" for poker players. Some of the material is outdated because games and game structures have changed, and players have improved. That said, you cannot call yourself a serious poker player if you haven't read this book. The section on no-limit hold'em is still the standard reference on the subject.

Card Player Magazine. 3140 S. Polaris Ave. #8, Las Vegas, NV 89102 (702-871-1720). *Card Player* is a twice monthly publication covering the poker scene around the world, as well as blackjack and sports betting. People such as Mike Caro and Bob Ciaffone are regular contributors. Owner/Editor Linda Johnson is a high stakes poker player herself, and she keeps a constant pulse on poker goings-on.

Caro, M. *Mike Caro's Book of Tells.* Caro's best book. It gives volumes of information on how to read "tells" — a poker player's unintended signals about the quality of his hand.

Cooke, R. with Bond, J. *RealPoker: The Cooke Collection.* MGI, 1999. This is a collection of Roy Cooke's articles from *Card Player* magazine. Roy's grammar is sometimes a bit awkward, and the book could have used a more thorough proofing. That said, you *must* read this book after you've been playing

---

[1]This book may be out of print now. Check your local library or used book store.

hold'em for a year or so. Roy has consistently beaten the very tough mid-limit Las Vegas games over many years, and, unlike most of the few others who have, knows how to describe what he does.

Harroch, R. and Krieger, L. *Poker For Dummies*. IDG Books, 2000. This is an excellent introductory text written in the "Dummies" books usual breezy style with many side bars and such.

Holden, A. *Big Deal*. Viking, 1990 (paperback version available). This is the *best* narrative book on poker ever written. Anthony Holden, a well known writer and serious poker player in the U.K., took a year off to be a professional poker player. This is his player's eye view of medium and high-limit games, as well as the big poker tournaments. Holden is a world-class writer, and you won't be able to put this book down. Read it after Alverez's *The Biggest Game In Town* for chronological reasons.

Krieger, L. *Hold'em Excellence*. ConJelCo, 2000. I can highly recommend Lou's book which, unlike most, is good for beginning hold'em players. His discussion of playing AK pre-flop is particularly important.

Malmuth, M. *Gambling Theory and Other Topics*. 2+2 Publishing, 1999. Mason Malmuth is one of the top theorists in poker today (as well as being an extremely strong mid-limit player). This book is a series of essays — some about poker, some about blackjack, and some about gambling in general. Anything Mason Malmuth writes is worth reading.

Malmuth, M. *Poker Essays*. 2+2 Publishing, 1991. More essays, all of these about poker. Mason is an intense, straightforward writer, and his essays are jam-packed with good information.

Sklansky, D. *Theory of Poker*. 2+2 Publishing, 1994. David Sklansky is another poker player/author who has written some of the seminal work on poker theory. This is probably the best book on poker ever written. First published in 1987, it has become a classic in the field. It is not easy reading, and you will want to read it after you've played a lot of poker. However, to quote

Sklansky himself, "If there's something I know about the game that the other person doesn't, and if he's not willing to learn or can't understand, then *I take his money.*"[2] Read this book.

Sklansky, D. and Malmuth, M. *Hold'em Poker for Advanced Players.* 2+2 Publishing, 1999. This is one of the "Advanced" series (they also have a book on seven card stud and a book by poker expert Ray Zee on high-low split games with an eight or better qualifier). Each book is considered the current reference for its game. Do not attempt to take on medium- or high-limit hold'em games without virtually memorizing this book.

---

[2]This quote is taken from Alvarez's book, *The Biggest Game in Town*, listed above.

Glossary

Action

(1) Opportunity to act. If a player appears not to realize it's his turn, the dealer will say "Your action, sir." (2) Bets and raises. "If a third heart hits the board and there's a lot of action, you have to assume that somebody has made the flush."

Ante

A small portion of a bet contributed by each player to seed the pot at the beginning of a poker hand. Most hold'em games do not have an ante; they use "blinds" to get initial money into the pot.

All-In

To run out of chips while betting or calling. In table stakes games, a player may not go into his pocket for more money during a hand. If he runs out, a side pot is created in which he has no interest. However, he can still win the pot for which he had the chips. Example: "Poor Bob. He made quads against the big full house, but he was all-in on the second bet."

Backdoor

Catching both the turn and river card to make a drawing hand. For instance, suppose you have A♠-7♠. The flop comes A♦-6♣-4♠. You bet and are called. The turn is the T♠, which everybody checks, and then the river is the J♠. You've made a "backdoor" nut flush. See also "runner."

Bad Beat

To have a hand that is a large underdog beat a heavily favored hand. It is generally used to imply that the winner of the pot had no business being in the pot at all, and it was the wildest of luck that he managed to catch the one card in the deck that would win the pot.

We won't give any examples; you will hear plenty of them during your poker career.

Big Blind The larger of the two blinds typically used in a hold'em game. The big blind is normally a full first round bet. See also "blind" and "small blind."

Blank A board card that doesn't seem to affect the standings in the hand. If the flop is A♠-J♦-T♠, then a turn card of 2♥ would be considered a blank. On the other hand, the 2♠ would *not* be.

Blind A forced bet (or partial bet) put in by one or more players before any cards are dealt. Typically, blinds are put in by players immediately to the left of the button. See also "live blind."

Board All the community cards in a hold'em game — the flop, turn, and river cards together. Example: "There wasn't a single heart on the board."

Bottom Pair A pair with the lowest card on the flop. If you have A♠-6♠, and the flop comes K♦-T♥-6♣, you have flopped bottom pair.

Burn To discard the top card from the deck, face down. This is done between each betting round before putting out the next community card(s). It is security against any player recognizing or glimpsing the next card to be used on the board.

Button A white acrylic disk that indicates the (nominal) dealer. Also used to refer to the player on the button. Example: "Oh, the button raised."

Buy (1) As in "buy the pot." To bluff, hoping to "buy" the pot without being called. (2) As in "buy the button." To bet or raise, hoping to make players between you and the button fold, thus allowing you to act last on subsequent betting rounds.

Call　To put into the pot an amount of money equal to the most recent bet or raise. The term "see" (as in "I'll see that bet") is considered colloquial.

Calling Station　A weak-passive player who calls a lot, but doesn't raise or fold much. This is the kind of player you like to have in your game.

Cap　To put in the last raise permitted on a betting round. This is typically the third or fourth raise. Dealers in California are fond of saying "Capitola" or "Cappuccino."

Case　The last card of a certain rank in the deck. Example: "The flop came J-8-3; I've got pocket jacks, he's got pocket 8's, and then the case eight falls on the river, and he beats my full house."[1]

Center Pot　The first pot created during a poker hand, as opposed to one or more "side" pots created if one or more players goes all-in. Also "main pot."

Check　(1) To not bet, with the option to call or raise later in the betting round. Equivalent to betting zero dollars. (2) Another word for chip, as in poker chip.

Check Raise　To check and then raise when a player behind you bets. Occasionally you will hear people say this is not fair or ethical poker. Piffle. Almost all casinos permit check-raising, and it

---

[1]See, there's your first bad beat story.

is an important poker tactic. It is particularly useful in low-limit hold'em where you need extra strength to narrow the field if you have the best hand.

Chop   An agreement between the two players with blinds to simply take their blinds back rather than playing out the hand if nobody calls or raises in front of them.

Cold Call   To call more than one bet in a single action. For instance, suppose the first player to act after the big blind raises. Now any player acting after that must call two bets "cold." This is different from calling a single bet and then calling a subsequent raise.

Come Hand   A drawing hand (probably from the craps term).

Complete Hand   A hand that is defined by all five cards — a straight, flush, full house, four of a kind, or straight flush.

Connector   A hold'em starting hand in which the two cards are one apart in rank. Examples: KQs, 76.

Counterfeit   To make your hand less valuable because of board cards that duplicate it. Example: you have 87 and the flop comes 9-T-J, so you have a straight. Now an 8 comes on the turn. This has counterfeited your hand and made it almost worthless.

Crack   To beat a hand — typically a big hand. You hear this most often applied to pocket aces: "Third time tonight I've had pocket aces cracked."[2]

---

[2]That's *two* bad-beat stories in this one chapter. See our point?

Cripple   As in "to cripple the deck." Meaning that you have most or all of the cards that somebody would want to have with the current board. If you have pocket kings, and the other two kings flop, you have crippled the deck.

Dog   Shortened form of "underdog."

Dominated Hand

A hand that will almost always lose to a better hand that people usually play. For instance, K3 is "dominated" by KQ. With the exception of strange flops (e.g., 3-3-X, K-3-X), it will always lose to KQ.

Draw   To play a hand that is not yet good, but could become so if the right cards come. Example: "I'm not there yet — I'm drawing." Also used as a noun. Example: "I have to call because I have a good draw."

Draw Dead   Trying to make a hand that, even if made, will not win the pot. If you're drawing to make a flush, and your opponent already has a full house, you are "drawing dead." Of course, this is a bad condition to be in.

Equity   Your "rightful" share of a pot. If the pot contains $80, and you have a 50% chance of winning it, you have $40 equity in the pot. This term is somewhat fanciful since you will either win $80 or $0, but it gives you an idea of how much you can "expect" to win.

Expectation   (1) The amount you expect to gain on average if you make a certain play. For instance, suppose you put $10 into a $50 pot to draw at a hand that you will make 25% of the time, and it will win every time you make it. Three out of four times, you do not make your draw, and lose $10 each time for a total of $30. The fourth time, you will make your draw, winning $50. Your total gain over those four average hands is $50-$30 = $20, an average of $5 per hand. Thus calling the $10 has a positive expectation of $5. (2) The amount you expect to make at the poker table in a specific time period. Suppose in 100 hours of play, you win $527. Then your expectation is $5.27/hr. Of course, you won't make that exact amount each hour (and some hours you will lose), but it's one measure of your *anticipated* earnings.

Extra Blind A blind put in by a player just entering the game, returning to the game, or otherwise changing his position at the table. See also "blind" and "post."

Family Pot A pot in which all (or almost all) of the players call before the flop.

Fast As in "play fast." To play a hand aggressively, betting and raising as much as possible. Example: "When you flop a set but there's a flush draw possible, you have to play it fast."[3]

Flop The first three community cards, put out face up, altogether.

Foul A hand that may not be played for one reason or another. A player with a foul hand may not make any claim on any portion of the pot. Ex-

---

[3]Please don't show this phrase to any English teachers. "Play" is a verb, and thus should be modified by an adverb; "fast" is an adjective. However, if you say "Play quickly" that usually implies that time is collected every half hour, and people want you to make your playing decisions without hesitation. "Play fast" is an idiom unique to poker.

ample: "He ended up with three cards after the flop, so the dealer declared his hand foul."

Free Card A turn or river card on which you don't have to call a bet because of play earlier in the hand (or because of your reputation with your opponents). For instance, if you are on the button and raise when you flop a flush draw, your opponents may check to you on the turn. If you make your flush on the turn, you can bet. If you don't get it on the turn, you can check as well, seeing the river card for "free."

Free Roll One player has a shot at winning an entire pot when he is currently tied with another player. For instance, suppose you have A♣-Q♣ and your opponent has A♦-Q♥. The flop is Q♠-5♣-T♣. You are tied with your opponent right now, but are free rolling, because you can win the whole pot and your opponent can't. If no club comes, you split the pot with him; if it does come, you win the whole thing.

Gutshot Straight

A straight filled "inside." If you have 9♠-8♠, the flop comes 7♣-5♥-2♦, and the turn is the 6♣, you've made your gutshot straight.

Heads Up A pot that is being contested by only two players. Example: "It was heads up by the turn."

Hit As in "the flop hit me," meaning the flop contains cards that help your hand. If you have AK, and the flop comes K-7-2, it hit you.

House The establishment running the game. Example: "The $2 you put on the button goes to the house."

Implied Odds

Pot odds that do not exist at the moment, but may be included in your calculations because of bets you expect to win if you hit your hand. For instance, you might call with a flush draw on the turn even though the pot isn't offering you quite 4:1 odds (your chance of making the flush) because you're sure you can win a bet from your opponent on the river if you make your flush.

Jackpot

A special bonus paid to the loser of a hand if he gets a very good hand beaten. In hold'em, the "loser" must typically get aces full or better beaten. In some of the large southern California card clubs, jackpots have gotten over $50,000. Of course, the jackpot is funded with money removed from the game as part of the rake.

Kicker

An unpaired card used to determine the better of two near-equivalent hands. For instance, suppose you have AK and your opponent has AQ. If the flop has an ace in it, you both have a pair of aces, but you have a king kicker. Kickers can be vitally important in hold'em.

Limp

To call. Generally the term refers to pre-flop action. For instance: "He limped in early position with 77."

Live Blind

A forced bet put in by one or more players before any cards are dealt. The "live" means those players still have the option of raising when the action gets back around to them.

Maniac

A player who does a lot of hyper-aggressive raising, betting, and bluffing. A true maniac is not a good player, but is simply doing a lot of gambling. However, a player who *occasion-*

ally acts like a maniac and confuses his opponents is quite dangerous.

Muck   The pile of folded and burned cards in front of the dealer. Example: "His hand hit the muck so the dealer ruled it folded even though the guy wanted to get his cards back." Also used as a verb. Example: He didn't have any outs so he mucked his hand."

No-Limit A version of poker in which a player may bet any amount of chips (up to the number in front of him) whenever it is his turn to act. It is a very different game from limit poker.

Nuts   The best possible hand given the board. If the board is K♠-J♦-T♠-4♠-2♥, then A♠-X♠ is the nuts. You will occasionally hear the term applied to the best possible hand of a certain category, even though it isn't the overall nuts. For the above example, somebody with A♥-Q♣ might say they had the "nut straight."

Offsuit   A hold'em starting hand with two cards of different suits.

One-Gap   A hold'em starting hand with two cards two apart in rank. Examples: J9s, 64.

Out   A card that will make your hand win. Normally heard in the plural. Example: "Any spade will make my flush, so I have nine outs."

Outrun   To beat. Example: "Susie outran my set when her flush card hit on the river."

Overcall To call a bet after one or more others players have already called.

Overcard A card higher than any card on the board. For instance, if you have AQ and the flop comes

J-7-3, you don't have a pair, but you have two overcards.

Overpair A pocket pair higher than any card on the flop. If you have QQ and the flop comes J-8-3, you have an overpair.

Pay Off To call a bet when the bettor is representing a hand that you can't beat, but the pot is sufficiently large to justify a call anyway. Example: "He played it exactly like he made the flush, but I had top set so I paid him off."

Play the Board To show down a hand in hold'em when your cards don't make a hand any better than is shown on the board. For instance, if you have 22, and the board is 4-4-9-9-A (no flush possible), then you must "play the board": the best possible hand you can make doesn't use any of your cards. Note that if you play the board, the best you can do is split the pot with all remaining players.

Pocket Your unique cards that only you can see. For instance, "He had pocket sixes" (a pair of sixes), or "I had ace-king in the pocket."

Pocket Pair A hold'em starting hand with two cards of the same rank, making a pair. Example: "I had big pocket pairs seven times in the first hour. What else can you ask for?"

Post To put in a blind bet, generally required when you first sit down in a cardroom game. You may also be required to post a blind if you change seats at the table in a way that moves you away from the blinds. Example: a player leaves one seat at a table and takes another in such a way that he moves farther from the blinds. He is required to *post* an extra blind to receive a hand. See also "extra blind."

Pot-limit   A version of poker in which a player may bet up to the amount of money in the pot whenever it is his turn to act. Like no-limit, this is a very different game from limit poker.

Pot Odds   The amount of money in the pot compared to the amount you must put in the pot to continue playing. For example, suppose there is $60 in the pot. Somebody bets $6, so the pot now contains $66. It costs you $6 to call, so your pot odds are 11:1. If your chance of having the best hand is at least 1 out of 12, you should call. Pot odds also apply to draws. For instance, suppose you have a draw to the nut flush with one card left to come. In this case, you are about a 4:1 underdog to make your flush. If it costs you $8 to call the bet, then there must be about $32 in the pot (including the most recent bet) to make your call correct.

Price   The pot odds you are getting for a draw or call. Example: "The pot was laying me a high enough price, so I stayed in with my gutshot straight draw."

Protect   (1) To keep your hand or a chip on your cards. This prevents them from being fouled by a discarded hand, or accidentally mucked by the dealer. (2) To invest more money in a pot so blind money that you've already put in isn't "wasted." Example: "He'll always protect his blinds, no matter how bad his cards are."

Put on   To mentally assign a hand to a player for the purposes of playing out your hand. Example:

"He raised on the flop, but I put him on a draw, so I re-raised and then bet the turn."

Quads	Four of a kind.
Ragged	A flop (or board) that doesn't appear to help anybody very much. A flop that came down J♦-6♥-2♣ would look ragged.
Rainbow	A flop that contains three different suits, thus no flush can be made on the turn. Can also mean a complete five card board that has no more than two of any suit, thus no flush is possible.
Rake	An amount of money taken out of every pot by the dealer. This is the cardroom's income.
Rank	The numerical value of a card (as opposed to its suit). Example: "jack," "seven."
Represent	To play as if you hold a certain hand. For instance, if you raised before the flop, and then raised again when the flop came ace high, you would be representing at least an ace with a good kicker.
Ring Game	A regular poker game as opposed to a tournament. Also referred to as a "live" game since actual money is in play instead of tournament chips.
River	The fifth and final community card, put out face up, by itself. Also known as "fifth street." Metaphors involving the river are some of poker's most treasured cliches, e.g., "He drowned in the river."
Rock	A player who plays very tight, not very creatively. He raises only with the best hands. A real rock is fairly predictable: if he raises you

on the end, you can throw away just about anything but the nuts.

Runner

Typically said "runner-runner" to describe a hand that was made only by catching the correct cards on both the turn and the river. Example: "He made a runner-runner flush to beat my trips." See also "backdoor."

Scare Card

A card that may well turn the best hand into trash. If you have T♣-8♣ and the flop comes Q♦-J♦-9♠, you almost assuredly have the best hand. However, a turn card of T♦ would be very scary because it would almost guarantee that you are now beaten.

Second Pair

A pair with the second highest card on the flop. If you have A♠-T♠, and the flop comes K♦-T♥-6♣, you have flopped second pair. See "top pair."

Sell

As in "sell a hand." In a spread-limit game, this means betting less than the maximum when you have a very strong hand, hoping players will call whereas they would not have called a maximum bet.

Semi-Bluff

A powerful concept first discussed by David Sklansky. It is a bet or raise that you hope will not be called, but you have some outs if it is. A semi-bluff may be correct when betting for value is not correct, a pure bluff is not correct, but the combination of the two may be a positive expectation play. Example: you have K♠-Q♠, and the flop is T♥-5♠-J♣. If you bet now, it's a semi-bluff. You probably don't have the best hand, and you'd like to see your opponents fold immediately. Nevertheless, if you do get callers, you could still improve to the best hand.

Set	Three of a kind when you have two of the rank in your hand, and there is one on the board.
Short Stack	A number of chips that is not very many compared to the other players at the table. If you have $10 in front of you, and everybody else at the table has over $100, you are playing on a short stack.
Showdown	The point at which all players remaining in the hand turn their cards over and determine who has the best hand — i.e. after the fourth round of betting is completed. Of course, if a final bet or raise is not called, there is no showdown.
Side Pot	A pot created in which a player has no interest because he has run out of chips. Example: Al bets $6, Beth calls the $6, and Carl calls, but he has only $2 left. An $8 side pot is created that either Al or Beth can win, but not Carl. Carl, however, can still win all the money in the original or "center" pot.
Slow Play	To play a strong hand weakly so more players will stay in the pot.
Small Blind	The smaller of two blind bets typically used in a hold'em game. Normally, the small blind is one-third to two-thirds of a first round bet. See also "big blind" and "blind."
Smooth Call	To call. Smooth call often implies slow playing a strong hand. Example: "I flopped the nut flush but just smooth called when the guy in front of me bet — I didn't want to scare anybody out."

Splash the pot[4] To toss chips directly into the pot rather than put them in a stack in front of you. Don't do it.

Split Pot A pot that is shared by two or more players because they have equivalent hands.

Split Two Pair

A two pair hand in which one of each of your cards' ranks appears on the board as well. Example: you have T9, the flop is T-9-5, you have a split two pair. This is in comparison to two pair where there is a pair on the board. Example: you have T9, the flop is 9-5-5.

Spread-limit A betting structure in which a player may bet any amount in a range on every betting round. A typical spread-limit structure is $2-$6, where a player may bet as little as $2 or as much as $6 on every betting round.

Straddle An optional extra blind bet, typically made by the player one to the left of the big blind, equal to twice the big blind. This is effectively a raise, and forces any player who wants to play to pay two bets. Furthermore, the straddler acts last before the flop, and may "re-raise."

String Bet A bet (more typically a raise) in which a player doesn't get all the chips required for the raise into the pot in one motion. Unless he verbally declared the raise, he can be forced to withdraw it and just call. This prevents the unethical play of putting out enough chips to

---

[4]This phrase is used delightfully in the John Dahl movie *Rounders*, one of the few films that accurately portrays poker action.

call, seeing what effect that had, and then possibly raising.

Structured   Used to apply to a certain betting structure in poker games. The typical definition of a structured hold'em game is a fixed amount for bets and raises before the flop and on the flop, and then twice that amount on the turn and river. Example: a $2-$4 structured hold'em game: bets and raises of $2 before the flop and on the flop; $4 bets and raises on the turn and river.

Suited   A hold'em starting hand in which the two cards arc the same suit. Example: "I *had* to play J-3 —it was suited."

Table Stakes   A rule in a poker game meaning that a player may not go into his pocket for money during a hand. He may only invest the amount of money in front of him into the current pot. If he runs out of chips during the hand, a side pot is created in which he has no interest. All casino poker is played table stakes. The definition sometimes also includes the rule that a player may not remove chips from the table during a game. While this rule might not be referred to as "table stakes," it is enforced almost universally in public poker games.

Tell   A clue or hint that a player unknowingly gives about the strength of his hand, his next action, etc. May originally be from "telegraph" or the obvious use that he "tells" you what he's going to do before he does it.

Thin   As in "drawing thin." To be drawing to a very few outs, perhaps only one or two.

Tilt	To play wildly or recklessly. A player is said to be "on tilt" if he is not playing his best, playing too many hands, trying wild bluffs, raising with bad hands, etc.
Time	(1) A request by a player to suspend play while he decides what he's going to do. Simply, "Time, please!" If a player doesn't request time and there is a substantial amount of action behind him, the dealer may rule that the player has folded. (2) An amount of money collected either on the button or every half hour by the cardroom. This is another way for the house to make its money (see "rake").
Toke	A small amount of money (typically $.50 or $1.00) given to the dealer by the winner of a pot. Quite often, tokes represent the great majority of a dealer's income.
Top Pair	A pair with the highest card on the flop. If you have A♠-Q♠, and the flop comes Q♦-T♥-6♣, you have flopped top pair. See "second pair."
Top Set	The highest possible trips. Example: you have T♣-T♠, and the flop comes T♦-8♣-9♥. You have flopped top set.
Top Two	Two pair, with your two hole cards pairing the two highest cards on the board.
Top and Bottom	Two pair, with your two hole cards pairing the highest and lowest cards on the board.
Trips	Three of a kind.
Turn	The fourth community card. Put out face up, by itself. Also known as "fourth street."
Under the Gun	The position of the player who acts first on a betting round. For instance, if you are one to

the left of the big blind, you are under the gun before the flop.

Underdog   A person or hand not mathematically favored to win a pot. For instance, if you flop four cards to your flush, you are not quite a 2:1 underdog to make your flush by the river (that is, you will make your flush about one in three times). See also "dog."

Value   As in "bet for value." This means that you would actually like your opponents to call your bet (as opposed to a bluff). Generally it's because you have the best hand. However, it can also be a draw that, given enough callers, has a positive expectation.

Variance   A measure of the up and down swings your bankroll goes through. Variance is not necessarily a measure of how well you play. However, the higher your variance, the wider swings you'll see in your bankroll.

Wheel   A straight from ace through five.

Index

A

Advancing to higher limits 4, 171
A-K 110
All-in
  intentionally getting 159
Alvarez, A. 173
Ante
  in hold'em games 13

B

Bad beat 166
  staying calm after a 166
Bankroll
  how much do you need? 159
  short stacks 159
Betting
  less than the maximum 148
  only when you want a call 128
  overcards 109
  the river 130
  with dominated hands 53
Big cards
  definition of 31
Blinds
  live 14
  structure of 13
Bluffing
  a short stacked player 160
  by maniacs 141
  when the flop misses you 112
  with a pair on the board 84
Board
  definition of 12

playing the 12
Brunson, Doyle 147, 173
Button
  advantage of being on 31
  definition of 13
  getting free play on the 51

C

Calling
  with big pairs pre-flop 39
  with marginal hands 126
Calling station 140
  recognizing a 142
Card Player magazine 7, 173
Cardrooms 3
  environment 164
  how game is played in 13
Caro, Mike 173
Casinos 3
  how game is played in 13
  playing in 162
Check-raise
  importance of 68, 151
  problem with the 71
  to get a free card 70
  with a draw 95
  with top pair 72
Computers in poker 151
Confrontations
  on the flop 116
Connectors
  definition of 31
Conventions 10

About the Author

In spite of being a consistent winner at low-limit Hold'em, Lee Jones still has to work for a living, so he is a Computer Aided Design programmer in Silicon Valley. He is delighted that he can now play cardroom poker smoke-free. He always enjoys local home games where there's no rake and you don't toke the dealers.

He got into poker about fourteen years ago[1], having studied blackjack a lot and discovering that you had to drive a long way from San Jose to play blackjack with pretty bad rules against a multi-billion dollar corporation that was determined to beat you. Poker is a much easier way to make money at cards.

Lee is a NAUI-certified scuba instructor, and spends as much time as possible teaching scuba in the Monterey area and diving all over the world. It turns out that in scuba diving, like poker, the idea is to find as many fish as possible.

His other interests include writing, ultimate Frisbee, trout fishing, and performing music.

He and his wife, Lisa, live in San Jose with Lisa's sons David and John. All four of them scuba dive, perform music, and play poker, so his life is pretty darn good.

---

[1]This is the first time I really figured out how long I've been playing poker seriously. Yikes.

About the Publisher

ConJelCo is a publisher based in Pittsburgh, Pennsylvania that specializes in books and software for the serious gambler. In addition to the book, *Winning Low-Limit Hold'em* by Lee Jones, ConJelCo publishes *Las Vegas Blackjack Diary* by Stuart Perry, *Video Poker—Optimum Play* by Dan Paymar, *Hold'em Excellence* by Lou Krieger, *More Hold'em Excellence* by Lou Krieger, *Serious Poker* by Dan Kimberg, *Blackjack Trainer* for the Macintosh and Windows, *Ken Elliott's CrapSim* for DOS, and *StatKing* for Windows.

ConJelCo periodically publishes a newsletter, *The Intelligent Gambler*, sent free to our customers. *The Intelligent Gambler* carries articles by our authors as well as other respected authors in the gambling community. In addition, it is the source of information about new ConJelCo products and special offers.

ConJelCo also sells books, software and videos from other publishers. If you'd like a free catalog or to be put on the mailing list for *The Intelligent Gambler* you can write to us at:

> ConJelCo LLC
> 1460 Bennington Ave.
> Pittsburgh, PA 15217-1139

Our phone number is 412-621-6040 (for orders in the US and Canada 800-492-9210), and our fax number is 412-621-6214.

ConJelCo is also on the Internet. You can send electronic mail to us at *orders@conjelco.com*. From the World Wide Web you can reach us at URL *http://www.conjelco.com*. On our web server you'll find a complete, annotated, ConJelCo catalog, demos of software by ConJelCo and others, and lots of other goodies for the interested gambler.